D0853463

MAN OF GOD
18 DAYS OF PROMISE

PROCLAMATIONS
RELEASING THE POWER
OF
GOD'S WORD

Written and compiled by
Pastor John & Diana Hagee
with Barbara Haley

©2006 by John Hagee and John Hagee Ministries. Written by John Hagee. Edited by Teresa Weaver, Kimberly A. Prochaska and Barbara Belcher. Produced by Tina Ketterling. Designed by Rudkin Productions, Boerne, Texas. No part of this book may be used or reproduced in any manner whatsoever without written permission, except in the case of brief quotations embodied in critical articles and reviews. For additional information write John Hagee Ministries, P.O. Box 1400, San Antonio, Texas 78295-1400. Unless otherwise noted, Scripture taken from the Amplified Bible, Old Testament, copyright © 1965, 1987 by The Zondervan Corporation. The Amplified Bible, New Testament, copyright © 1954, 1958, 1987 by The Lockman Foundation. Used by permission of The Zondervan Corporation. All rights reserved.

ISBN#1-56908-024-0
PRINTED IN CHINA

Table o

Contents

Part Three – Scripture Verses

Notes (page 208)

The Power of Proclamation

To proclaim is to make known publicly your opinions, and to extol or praise an action or individual. To make a proclamation is to announce or declare, in an official or formal manner; as in proclaiming war![1]

It is a good and delightful thing

*to give thanks to the Lord,
to sing praises [with musical
accompaniment] to Your name,
O Most High, to show forth
Your loving-kindness in the
morning and Your faithfulness
by night. Psalm 92:1-2*

*But I trusted in, relied on and
was confident in You, O Lord;
I said, "You are my God!"
Psalm 31:14*

*Contend, O Lord, with those
who contend with me; fight
against those who fight against
me! Take hold of shield and
buckler, and stand up for my
help! Draw out also the spear
and javelin and close up the
way of those who pursue and
persecute me. Say to me, I am
your deliverance! Psalm 35:1-3*

The King of Kings and Lord of Lords has
redeemed us—we are His! Our heavenly
Father gave us His written Word as an
inheritance, a diary, a guidebook to what

He has done, what He has promised, and what He will do!

Christ Jesus who died... more than that, who was raised to life again... is at the right hand of God, the Father and is interceding for us. All we must do is to believe, obey and proclaim what the Spirit of the Living God, the God of Abraham, Isaac and Jacob has written.

We must take ownership of the Word of God. We must declare God's position over every situation in our lives. The phrase "to proclaim" comes from the Latin, which means to "shout forth." It is a strong word and is linked to another dynamic phrase or word in the New Testament... "to confess." Confession means to say the same with our mouths what God has already said in His Word.

We are to proclaim our victory over the flesh, the mind and the devil, because we are overcomers by the Blood of the Lamb and the word of our testimony. God's power is released in the supernatural when we speak His Word over our lives. That which is released in the supernatural affects the physical, where we live.

Jesus is the High Priest of our confession. Whenever we say with our mouths, what the Bible says about us as believers in Jesus, then we have released His authority and blessings over our proclamations.[2]

We must learn to magnify the Lord in all things. Instead, we usually magnify the obstacles in our lives. These challenges will overwhelm and defeat us if we focus on them. Yet the Lord has already defeated the enemy and provided the solution for our problems. Imagine a magnifying glass that a child looks through to find the ant crawling across the ground. The ant looks so big it frightens the child for fear the small insect will bring him or her harm. Yet this same glass when pointed toward the sun's rays will burn the ant to an ash.

God tells us to "fret not." Therefore, do not focus on the obstacles. Instead, magnify the God of Promise, Who has answers for every trouble you encounter. Focus on the Author of life and Giver of every perfect gift. Praise Him and Proclaim His awesome Word. Your issues did not take God by surprise and He has already provided a way for us to overcome life's challenges.

You must do more than believe the Word of the living God; you must also obey it; you must proclaim it over your life and the lives of your loved ones and you must have hope in the power of His promises. Anyone can believe; demons believe. The Word of God says that demons tremble at the mention of the name of the Lord. However, demons can't obey and they don't proclaim the Word over their lives; but you can!

When you have trust in Christ who is our Blessed Hope, then you can see the invisible, you can feel the intangible and you can accomplish the impossible! Be more than a conqueror–learn to be an overcomer for the God of Israel is on your side!

Lord, I pray this day that my life will be built and formed on Your Holy Word. Let it be my daily bread that strengthens me as I meditate on it day and night. Help me never to depart from it. Give me a hunger and passion for Your Word. Help me to do what Your Word says to do; then I will know that it is You, O Lord, that makes my way prosper and I will have good success. Thank you Lord that Your Word will never change and be forevermore. (2 Tim. 3:16,17)

The King's Protocol

There is a protocol or ceremonial form and courtesy followed when entering into the presence of those in authority such as judges, heads of state and most importantly the God of Abraham, Isaac and Jacob.

The protocol followed when entering the presence of God, our Father, is to affirm that you are His child. To do this, we must first acknowledge our sinful state *(Romans 3:23)*, confess our sins *(Psalm 32:5)*, repent of them and ask forgiveness *(Matthew 3:2)* and finally turn from our sinful state *(John 8:11)*.

All of us must personally accept Christ through the sinner's prayer; there are no exceptions! The most important decision you will ever make is to confess Jesus Christ as your Lord and Savior. If you have not prayed the prayer or are not sure, I encourage you to do so now.

Lord, I confess that I am a sinner. I have sinned and today I ask that You forgive me of all my sins, both known and unknown. Father, I ask that You accept me as Your own and write my name in the Lamb's Book of Life. I acknowledge that Jesus Christ, Your Son paid the price at Calvary for my salvation. Because of the Blood of the Cross, I am now

*forgiven and redeemed. My sins
are buried in the sea of forget-
fulness, never to be remembered
against me anymore. From this
day forward I will read and
obey Your Word. I am now a
child of God, a son of the King,
and Jesus Christ is the Lord of
my life. Amen.
(Romans 3:23, Romans 10:9,
Psalm 32:5, John 8:11, Micah
7:18-20, John 1:12).*

Secondly, one of the most important things you will learn to do as a child of the King is to forgive. For the Word says we are forgiven as we forgive others. Forgiveness is such an important key to living a victorious and abundant life and is often ignored by so many. We must never make the mistake of being held captive by the lack of forgiveness one for the other. Choose today to have a forgiving spirit and walk in the liberty that forgiveness affords.

We often have no problem forgiving others but we have great difficulty forgiving ourselves. Remember this truth; once we have been forgiven by God our Father, He has forgotten our sins. He has buried our offenses under the deepest sea never to be remembered. He, Who is All-Knowing and All-Powerful, says, He can't remember our transgressions; so you should forget them as well.

Father, I acknowledge that forgiveness is Your commandment, and I know that I should forgive others just as You have forgiven me. Help me forgive those who have injured me, and deliver me from the traps of anger and bitterness. Help me forgive myself as You have so mercifully forgiven me so that I may put my past behind me and begin anew. Forgiveness is Your way Lord; let it be mine.
(Ephesians 4:32, 1 John 1:9, Nehemiah 9:17)

Lastly, we must know and understand the Great Exchange made at the cross on our behalf.

Jesus was punished that we might be forgiven.

Jesus was wounded that we might be healed.

Jesus was made sin with our sinfulness that we might be made righteous with His righteousness.

Jesus died our death that we might receive His life.

Jesus was made a curse that we might enter into His blessing.

Jesus endured poverty that we might share His abundance.

Jesus bore our shame that we might share His glory.

Jesus endured rejection that we might have His acceptance with the Father.

Jesus was cut off by death that we might be joined to God eternally.

Our old man was put to death in Him that the new man might come to life in us.[3]

The King's Armor

We are fighting in a war and must learn to fight equipped with the armaments of war! Every morning as we prepare for the day we need to dress in the Armor of God before going out into the world's battlefield. A naked, unarmed soldier is not a threat to the enemy *(Ephesians 6:11).*

Father, today I dress myself in the

whole Armor of God having done all I stand, putting on:

The Helmet of Salvation – hope. The helmet will keep me from being double-minded. Let the mind that is in Christ Jesus be in me, that I may cast down all vain imaginations and take captive every idle thought. Protect my ears Lord, to hear only the voice of my Father and not the lies of the enemy. I put on the mind of Christ Jesus that I may be conformed to His image. I choose today to think on whatever is noble, just, pure, lovely, of a good report; if there is any virtue and anything praiseworthy I will think on these things. The helmet of Salvation is hope and Jesus Christ is my Blessed Hope. *(Jam.1:6-8; Isa.55:2; 2Cor.10:5; Mat.12:36; Phi.2:5; Eph.4:23; Rom.8:29; Phi.3:10-11; 4:8)*

The Breastplate of Righteousness – When I surrendered to the cross of my Savior, I was wrapped in the white robe of Jesus Christ Who is all righteousness; it is my breastplate. It will protect my heart, which is the wellspring of life. Blessed am I because I seek You with my whole heart. I will hide Your Word in my heart that I will not sin against You. I choose to have a pure heart set upon You Lord. *(Psa.119:2,11)*

The Belt/Girdle of Truth – You Father, are Truth, Your Word is Truth. Jesus, my Savior is the Way, the Truth and the Life. I walk in the truth of who I am in Christ Jesus. I am a lover of Truth for it has set me free. *(Joh.8:32;14:6; 17:17; Eph.4:21)*

The Shoes of the Gospel – The Gospel of Christ is The Good News. I walk in the knowledge that God so loved the world He sent His Son, Jesus Christ and because of His obedience, I will have a life of abundance–joy, peace, love, provision, health. I will not be ashamed of the Gospel of the Lord that I serve. *(Joh.3:16; Gal.5:22; Gen.1:26)*

The Shield of Faith – The Shield of Faith quenches the fiery darts of the evil one. The Lord is my shield and buckler. You are an ever-present help in the time of trouble. You are the lifter of my head. The name of the Lord is a strong tower and the righteous run into it and they are saved. The favor of God surrounds the righteous; therefore it surrounds me as a shield. You are my Shield, and my exceedingly Great Reward. *(Gen.1:15; Eph.6:16; Psa.91:4;119:114)*

The Sword of the Spirit – The Word of God is more powerful and sharper than any two-edged sword. The Sword of the Living God will pierce the darkness allowing light to penetrate, bringing repentance, healing and restoration. The Sword of the Spirit will divide the soul and spirit, the joints and marrow, the thoughts and intent of the heart to bring wholeness to my life. *(Heb.4:12; 2Cor.5:19)*

Unceasing Prayer – I will lift up the saints and bless them in the name of the Lord. I will pray for them without ceasing that He will be their protector, provider, and the lifter of their heads. Father, bless them that call you Lord! *(Isa.54:17; Eph. 6:18)*

Lord, today I choose to obey your commandments and walk after You. You go before me, for the steps of the righteous are ordered of God and today I walk on the path You have set before me. I am dressed in the Armor of God that I will stand and having done all I stand, for I know the battle is not mine; it belongs to You. You disarmed Satan at the Cross and he has no power over me. I praise You as I witness Your power and faithfulness in my life today! I am more than a conqueror I am an overcomer through YOU! *(Deu. 28:1-2; Psa. 37:23; Eph. 6:10-13; 2Chr. 20:15, 17,21-22; Col. 2:14-15; Rom.8:37-38)*

The Promises of God

God's promises can be considered as spiritual certificates of deposit and we are spiritual heirs to these deposits. Christ has paid the price for us at the Cross and allows us to present our drafts—these promises—to claim that which God has promised to provide. In return, we receive the great blessings God has pledged to us, by, through, and on account of His Son, Jesus Christ.[3]

GOD'S PROMISES COME WITH CONDITIONS

1. His promises belong only to those who are children of God through faith; heirs according to His Word. They belong to those who have surrendered their lives to Christ and been cleansed in His blood. They belong to those who have joined into a spiritual union with Christ and have clothed themselves with His robe of Righteousness.

> *For you are all sons of God through faith in Christ Jesus. For as many of you as were baptized into Christ have put on Christ. There is neither Jew nor Greek, there is neither slave nor free, there is neither male nor female; for you are all one in Christ Jesus. And if you are Christ's, then you*

*are Abraham's seed, and
heirs according to the promise.*
Galatians 3:26-29

2. God's promises are given on condition
   of our willingness to listen to His voice
   and obey His commands.

*If you will listen diligently to
the voice of the Lord your God,
being watchful to follow all His
commandments, which I command you this day, the Lord
your God will set you high above
all the nations of the earth.
And all these blessings shall
come upon you and overtake you
if you heed the voice of the Lord
your God.* *Deuteronomy 28:1-2*

We know that the promises are only
for His children, and we must keep
His commands in order to receive
His promises. This truth is confirmed
in the teaching in 1 John.

Now by this we know that we know Him, if we keep His commandments. He who says, "I know Him," and does not keep His commandments, is a liar, and the Truth is not in him. But whoever keeps His Word, truly the love of God is perfected in him. By this we know that we are in Him. 1 John 2:3-5

3. Many of God's promises are based on other specified conditions. Take for example, God's promise of peace. The condition assigned to us is that we must not worry.

Be anxious for nothing, but in everything by prayer and supplications, with thanksgiving, let your requests be made known to God; and the peace of God, which surpasses all understanding, will guard your hearts and minds through Christ Jesus.
Philippians 4:6-7

Consider the promise of God's presence in your life. The condition applied to us is that we must come closer to Him.

Come close to God, and He will come close to you. James 4:8

4. God's promises are given on condition of our faith and our choice to believe in them.

But let him ask in faith, with no doubting, for he who doubts is like a wave of the sea driven and tossed by the wind. For let not that man suppose that he will receive anything from the Lord. James 1:6-7

Therefore I say to you, whatever things you ask when you pray, believe that you will receive them, and you will have them. Mark 11:24

GOD CALLS US TO HIS PROMISES

He instructs us to study the Scriptures diligently to know and understand His will and promise for our lives.

> *Be diligent to present yourself approved to God, a worker who does not need to be ashamed, rightly dividing the word of truth.*   2 Timothy 2:15

His promises are made to be taken by His children, by all who will believe and claim them. "They were not made to lay concealed in a gilt-edged Bible, but to be read, understood and used. The fact is, the Bible is like a checkbook given to the needy, and we are to use it when we want to make a withdrawal from our Promise account. God has given promises to every kind and description of person; and these promises were given not to be hoarded up, but to be used — we are to draw liberally and freely upon the

Divine bounty for all the blessing that we need." [4]

The Journey

We are now ready to embark on a journey with the Lord Jesus Christ. We must remember that He is our Redeemer.

The body is a temple for the Holy Spirit – redeemed, cleansed, and sanctified by the blood of Jesus.

The parts of the body are instruments

of righteousness, yielded to God for His service and for His glory.

The devil has no place in you, no power over you, no unsettled claims against you.

All has been settled by the blood of Jesus. Practice these statements:

I overcome Satan by the blood of the Lamb and by the word of my testimony, and I do not love my life to the death.

My body is for the Lord and the Lord is for my body.[5]

We are to glean in His field. Our Redeemer's fields are filled with His promises and He wants us to gather all we can. God has promised never to leave us or forsake us. We must believe that promise! Jesus has promised to uphold us. We must believe Him when He says so. Jesus has promised to grant us victory over all our spiritual enemies. We must trust in His truthfulness. God is as good as His Word and He will do all that

He has promised.[6] Enjoy your journey. Partake of God's goodness and learn to abide in God's Promise Fields.

ADDICTIONS

God broke the power of _____ in my life when I surrendered completely to His will and direction. Because I once rebelled against the words of God and spurned the counsel of the Most High, I sat in darkness and bondage. I stumbled and fell, and no one was there to help. But when I cried out to the Lord in my trouble, He heard me and saved me from my distress. In His goodness and loving-kindness, He brought me out of darkness and shattered the bonds that held me. By His Word, I am healed!

I am a new creation in Christ Jesus. My old person was nailed to the cross with Christ in order that my body, the instrument of sin, might be made ineffective and inactive for evil. I am no longer a slave to sin, having been delivered from its power when I was crucified with Christ. The life I now live, I live by faith in the Son of God, Who loves me and gave His life for me.

I walk in the Truth, and the Truth has set me free! I am filled with the Holy Spirit and exercise the fruit of self-control in my life. The grace of God, that delivered me from sin, is training me as I reject and renounce all ungodliness and worldly desires, and live a humble, self-controlled, upright and spiritually whole life in this present world.

I no longer need _____, for God supplies all my needs according to His riches and glory in Christ Jesus. Because I belong to God, I am able to defeat and overcome evil. As I submit to God, I resist the devil, and he flees. For He who lives in me is mightier than he

who is in the world, and when I come
close to God, He comes close to me.
Christ empowers me with strength to do
all things. With faith in God's promises,
I vow to never again yield my body to
its cravings, subject to its lusts or evil
desires. I confidently walk as a servant
of righteousness—conforming my life to
God's divine will in thought, purpose
and action. I am victorious because my
faith is in Christ. I believe He is the Son
of God, and I place my hope and trust in
Him alone.

In obedience to the Word of God,
I abstain from the sensual urges, evil
desires, and passions of the flesh that
wage war with my soul, my mind, and
my body. I strip myself of my former
nature, corrupted through lusts and evil
desires. I no longer set my mind on
things that gratify the flesh, and am no
longer controlled by the unholy desires of
my flesh. I renounce the lust of my flesh,
the lust of my eyes, and the pride in my

life, for these do not come from God but are from the world itself.

Instead, I put on the new nature, created in God's image, in true righteousness and holiness. My new spiritual self is ever in the process of being renewed after the image and likeness of God. I am constantly renewed in the spirit of my mind by concentrating on and seeking those things that gratify the Holy Spirit. I am led by the desires of the Spirit, for the Holy Spirit lives within me to direct and control me.

Christ came that I might have and enjoy abundant life. Whereas, Satan comes to steal, kill and destroy. I steep myself in the Word of God that I might know the divine power that is mine in Christ's name. I meditate on His commands day and night to keep myself from sin, and I remain cautious at all times— on the lookout for Satan's attempts to lead me astray.

Jesus was made to be like me in every way, in order that He might become a sympathetic and faithful High Priest. He Himself suffered by being tempted in all things — tested and tried. Because of this, He, therefore, immediately runs to the sound of my cry when I am tempted, tested or tried. He knows how to rescue the godly, no matter the situation, out of temptations and trials. So then, I fearlessly, confidently and boldly draw near to Him and receive mercy and grace to help in times of trouble.

I walk in faith, not fear, for God is with me. He will never forsake me. He strengthens and helps me and makes the darkness into light before me. I ask, and God places a hedge of protection around me. He is my refuge and dwelling place. He drives the enemy out before me. Though I walk in the midst of trouble, He revives me — through the valley of the shadow of death, He is with me. He stretches out His hand against the wrath of my enemies, and His right hand saves me.

I test all things until I recognize that which is good; then I grasp it tightly in my hand. I will not be overcome by evil, but will overcome evil with good. I no longer try to fit into this world, but am transformed by the renewal of my mind. In this way I can rightly discern what the good, acceptable and perfect will of God is for me. Christ has set me free from the grips of addiction and sin. I determine in my heart, by the grace of God, to stand fast. I will never again be ensnared by the yoke of slavery to sin.

(Rom.6:17-18; Psa.107:8-14,20; 2Co.5:17; Rom.6:6-7; Gal.2:20; Joh.8:31-32; Gal.5:22-23; Tit.2:11-12; Phi.4:19; 1Jo.4:4; Jam.4:7-8; Phi.4:13; Rom.6:12-13, 17-18; 1Jo.5:4-5; 1Pe.2:11; Eph.4:22; Rom.8:5; 1Jo.2:16; Eph.4:24; Col.3:10; Rom.8:5,9; Joh.10:10; Act.20:32; Psa.119:11; 1Pe.5:8; Heb.2:17-18; 2Pe.2:9; Heb.4:16; Isa.41:10; 42:16; Joh.15:7; Job 1:9-10; Deu.33:27; Psa.23:4; 138:7; Rom.12:21; 1Th.5:21; Rom.12:2; Gal.5:1)

AUTHORITY

In obedience to God's Word, I offer up prayer and thanksgiving for all who are in positions of authority. I speak blessings over them and pray that they might be saved and increasingly able to perceive and know how to precisely and accurately handle the divine Truth of God. I pray that God will teach our leaders to do His will and that He will send His Spirit to guide our leaders to further His cause—for this will elevate our nation. I pray that God will lead those in authority to live a noble life, acting honorably and in complete honesty in all things, and that He will speak His Word over their lives. For His Word does not return to Him void, without producing any effect. Rather, it accomplishes His purpose and pleasure and prospers in the thing for which He sends it.

All authority comes from God, existing only by His permission and appointment.

Christ is the head of all who rule and carry authority. They are God's servants for my good; I am loyally subject and submissive to them. I do not fear those in authority because I conduct myself in a way that is pleasing to God. I do what is right to show that I can be fully trusted, so that in every way I make the teaching about God, my Savior, more attractive. In accordance to the Word of God, I am submissive to authority for the sake of the Lord. In reverence to God, I honor and show respect at all times for those in authority over me, regardless of their words, attitudes or behavior.

God fills me with wisdom, strength and favor when I have the opportunity to come before those in authority as a testimony to them for the Lord's sake. I am not anxious about how or what I say; I am given what to say as I need it. For it is not me speaking, but the Holy Spirit speaking through me.

I shine with God's light and will let His light shine through me so those in authority will see my moral fiber and recognize, praise and glorify my Father, Who is in heaven. As a child of God, who is called by His name, I humble myself, pray and seek God's face, turning from my wicked ways; God hears from heaven, forgives my sins, and heals my land.

(1Ti.2:1-4; Psa.143:10; Pro.14:34; Heb.13:18; 4:12; Isa. 55:1; Rom.13:1; Col.2:10; Rom.13:3-4; Tit.2:9-10; 1Pe.2:13, 17-18; Mat.10:18-20; 5:14,16; 2Ch.7:14)

BLESSINGS—SPIRITUAL

I am blessed, for my sins have been forgiven and covered by the Lord that I serve. I am blessed as I seek Him with my whole heart. Out of His abundance I have received one grace after another, spiritual blessing upon spiritual blessing, favor upon favor, and gift upon gift. I will receive showers of blessings from the God of Abraham, Isaac and Jacob. Because I believe in Christ, I have the blessing of

Abraham and, through faith, receive the promise of the Holy Spirit. I am blessed in Christ with every spiritual blessing in the heavenly realm.

(Psa.32:1; 119:2; Joh.1:16; Eze.34:26; Gal.3:14; Eph.1:3)

BLESSINGS—MATERIAL

Because I have received Jesus Christ into my heart and life, the blessing promised to Abraham has come upon me. I am in Christ as Abraham's seed, and, therefore, an heir of the promised blessing. As I hear and do His Word, God will keep me, love me and multiply me. He blesses the fruit of my body, the fruit of my land, and all that He has provided for me. I am blessed above all others. As I keep His commandments, God's blessings overtake me and I am blessed in the city and in the field; blessed is the fruit of my body, the fruit of my ground, and the fruit of my livestock. I am blessed in my basket and my storehouse will be full. I am blessed coming in and going out. The Lord will bless all I undertake. When I do all that my Lord commands, I am the head and not the tail. God blesses me as He yields His harvest, and I, and all the earth, reverently fear Him.

(Deu.7:12-14; 28:1-13; Psa.67:6; Gal.3:14,29)

THE BLOOD OF CHRIST

The blood of the Lamb is on the doorposts of my soul; therefore, no plague shall enter into my spirit and destroy me. I have partaken of the Blood of the Lamb that was shed for the remission of my sins. I will examine myself so that I may be worthy of taking the cup of the Lord. I have redemption and have been purified through the blood of Christ, Who gave Himself as a sacrifice for my transgressions. This same blood seals the covenant that I have with the King of Kings and the

Lord of Lords. I have been redeemed from my past and traditions and have been purchased with neither silver nor gold, but with the precious blood of Christ. I have been brought near to the Father by the blood of His Son, and cleansed of all sin and guilt.

(Exo.12:13; Mat.26:27; 1Co.11:28; Eph.1:7; 2:13; Heb.9:14,20; 1Pe.1:18-19; 1Jo.1:7)

CHILDREN

My children are a heritage of the Lord, and I am happy, blessed and fortunate to have them. They were wonderfully and fearfully knit together by God in the womb. Their frame was not hidden from Him as He intricately formed them in secret as if embroidering with various colors. Because I listen closely to the voice of God and faithfully keep His commands, my children are blessed of God. He is with them wherever they go, leading them and holding them in His right hand.

As an heir to the promise of Abraham, I speak health to my children's bodies, pray a hedge of protection around them, and claim God's hand of prosperity and happiness upon the work of their hands. And I bind Satan in the mighty Name of Jesus. By the authority of the Blood of the Lamb, I cancel any assignment Satan might have against my children. I will not fear because God guards and keeps my children and gives them His peace.

I pray constantly for my children, that God will continuously strengthen and reinforce them with mighty power, as the Holy Spirit takes up residence in their innermost beings and personalities. I pray that His power might enable them to grasp and come to know, through personal experience, the love of Christ, which goes beyond simple knowledge. I pray that they might become rooted and

securely founded in His love, flooded
with the divine Presence of God Himself.

*(Ps.127:3,5, 139:13-15; Dt.28:1-4; Ps.139:7-10;
Dt.7:12-15; Job1:10; Mat.18:18; Ps.12:7; Num.6:24,26;
Eph.3:16-19)*

DISCERNMENT

The Holy Spirit guides me into the full
Truth—that is, Jesus Christ—Who speaks
not His own message, but the message
the Father has given Him. I saturate
myself in the Word of God because it
is alive and full of power—sharper than
any two-edged sword, exposing, sifting,
analyzing and judging the very thoughts
and purposes of my heart. God's Word
gives me light, discernment and compre-
hension. I pray believing that the Lord
fills me with a deep and clear knowledge
of His will and the ability to discern spiritual matters. I discern between good and
evil and choose for myself that which is
right. I take no part in evil, but instead,
strive to live my life in such contrast as to

expose and convict the deeds of darkness. I have surrendered my heart to God and submitted to His will, for He desires that I recognize and correctly discern the divine Truth.

I meditate on the Proverbs. God has given them to me that I might gain Godly Wisdom and be able to discern and comprehend words of insight and understanding. My reverent worship and fear of the Lord produces knowledge, which I store up in my mind and heart. I do not let wisdom and discernment escape from my sight because they are life to my inner self and a gracious ornament to my outer self. I walk in security and confident trust; I do not dash my foot or stumble. When I lie down, I am not afraid, and I sleep soundly.

God discerns and understands my thoughts from a distance. He searches my heart and reveals the deep and secret things contained within. When I listen to

His voice and confess my sin to God, not trying to hide it, He instantly forgives me and cleanses my heart from all unrighteousness. God's love has been poured into my heart through the Holy Spirit, and as it abounds, I am able to discern what is vital—the highest and the best. I prize that which is excellent, so that, without stumbling or causing others to stumble, I keep my heart sincere and pure until Christ returns.

(Joh.16:13; Heb.4:12; Psa.119:130; Mat.21:22; Col.1:9; Eph.5:11; 1Ti.2:4; Pro.1:1-2; 1:7; 10:14; 3:21-24; Psa.139:2; 23-24; Dan.2:22; Psa.32:5; 1Jo.1:9; Rom.5:5; Phi.1:9-10)

EMOTIONAL HEALTH

When the righteous cry for help, the Lord hears and delivers them out of all their distress and troubles. Therefore, You hear me when I cry out to You! You are close to the brokenhearted. You promise to bind up my wounds and heal my afflictions.

When my heart aches, I cry out to God, for He is near. He knows the secrets of my heart and is full of loving compassion. His understanding is unlimited. The Lord of peace grants me His peace at all times and in all ways. You are my Shepherd; You gather me in Your arms and carry me in Your bosom. You are always with me and will never leave me nor forsake me. Absolutely nothing can separate me from Your love.

When difficulties come and I cannot sleep for the bitterness of my soul, God loves me back from the pit. When I confess my sins, He cleanses me of my unrighteousness. The God of peace has crushed Satan under my feet; the grace of my Lord, Jesus Christ, is with me. He softens my hardened heart and gives me a heart that is sensitive and responsive to the touch of God.

A calm and undisturbed mind and heart are the life and health of my body. I will not allow my heart and mind to stay troubled, anxious or afraid. I ask You, Lord God, to search my heart, try my thoughts, and expose any wickedness or hurt within me. I will not allow myself to become angry and disturbed or permit myself to be fearful, intimidated or unsettled, for I am a victorious child of God. I am more than a conqueror through Him Who loves me. God did not give me a spirit of timidity or fear, but a spirit of power and love, a calm mind, discipline and self-control.

Though feelings such as fear, anxiety, rejection, anger, discouragement and depression are completely normal and to be expected, I will not allow them to control my attitude or behavior, for I am responsive to and controlled by the Holy Spirit, and the mind of the Spirit is life and peace.

With Your help, I will examine my feelings to uncover the faulty thoughts on which they are based, for as I think in my heart, so am I. I examine every thought that enters my mind, and I refuse to consider, believe or dwell on any argument or reasoning that contradicts the Word of God. With the help of the Holy Spirit, I speak the Word of God over my life. For God's Word promises protection and peace in times of fear and anxiety, unconditional love and unconditional acceptance in times of rejection, understanding and forgiveness in times of anger, faith and hope in times of discouragement, and compassion and healing in times of depression.

I continually bring my thoughts and needs to God in prayer. I thank Him for His love and His mercy, and His promise to affectionately care for me when I cast my cares on Him. And God's peace, which goes far beyond anything I could ever understand, settles over me, guarding my heart and mind in Christ Jesus.

I have the mind of Christ, holding the thoughts, feelings and purposes of His heart, and I set my mind on higher things. God keeps me in perfect and constant peace because I set my mind on Him. His eyes are on me, and His ears are attentive to my prayers. He watches to show Himself strong on my behalf. I put my trust in Him, for He is a very present help in trouble.

Bless me with Your smile and fill me with Your peace, oh Lord!

(Psa.34:17-18; 147:3; 145:18; 44:21; 111:4; 147:5; 2Th.3:16; Isa.40:11; Jos.1:5; Rom.8:38-39; Isa.38:15-16; 1Jo.1:9; Rom.16:20; Eze.11:19; Pro.14:30; Phi.4:6; Psa.139:23-24; Joh.14:27; Rom.8:37; 2Ti.1:7; Gal.5:16; Rom.8:6; Pro.23:7; 2Co.10:5; Isa.41:10; Rom.5:8; 2:11; Psa.27:10; Eph.4:31-32; Mat.17:20; Psa.33:20-22; Heb.4:13-16; Psa.30:2; 1Pe.5:7; Phi.4:6-7; 1Co.2:16; Col.3:2; Isa.26:3; 1Pe.3:12; 2Ch.16:9; Psa.56:11; 46:1; Num.6:26)

FAITHFULNESS

My God is a faithful God, keeping His covenant and steadfast love and mercy to all who love Him and keep His commandments. You are the Lord Who does not change. You are the same–yesterday, today and forever. Your faithfulness does not depend on me. Even when I do not believe, or when I stumble and become unfaithful to You, You remain faithful to Your Word and Your righteous character. You are my Rock. Your work is perfect, and Your ways are just and right.

I am happy, blessed and fortunate because God is my helper. He has made heaven and earth, the sea, and all that is in them, and is faithful forever. He shows me His loving-kindness in the morning and His faithfulness by night.

God's divine power provides me with all I need for life and godliness, through my personal knowledge of Him. He gives me His precious and exceedingly great promises, so that I am able, through them, to escape the corruption and moral decay in the world today. His Word goes forth from His mouth, and does not return empty—without producing any effect. Rather, it accomplishes exactly that for which He sends it. You, O Lord, are my hiding place and my shield. I place my hope in You, for Your promises are faithful to Your Word.

(Deu.7:9; Mal.3:6; Heb.13:8; Rom.3:3-4; 2Ti.2:13; Deu.32:4; Psa.146:5-6, 92:2; 2Pe.1:3-4; Isa.55:11; Psa.119:114; Heb.10:23)

FAVOR OF GOD

In the name of Jesus, I am the righteousness of God; therefore I am entitled to covenant kindness and favor. The favor of God is among the righteous. His favor surrounds the righteous; therefore, it surrounds me. I expect the favor of God to be in manifestation everywhere I go and in everything I do. Never again will I be without the favor of God.

Satan, my days in Lodebar cease today. I am leaving that place of lack and want.

I am going from the pit to the palace because the favor of God rests richly on me and profusely abounds in me. I am part of the generation that will experience the immeasurable, limitless and unsurpassed favor of God. This will produce in my life supernatural increase, promotion, prominence, preferential treatment, restoration, honor, increased assets, great victories, recognition, petitions granted, policies and rules changed on my behalf and battles won that I don't have to fight. The favor of God is upon me; it goes before me, and therefore, my life will never be the same.

(1Co.1:30; Act.3:25; Psa.5:12; 97:11; 1Ti.1:14; Col.2:15; Joh.10:10; Deu.28:1-13; Psa.112:1-4; Psa.84:11-12; Gen. 39:21; Ex. 3:21; 11:3; Dt. 33:23; 2 Chr. 20:15,29; 1 Sa. 16:22; Es. 2:17; 5:8; 8:5,8; Psa. 44:3)

FINANCES

I am blessed because I believe in, trust in and rely on the Lord, placing my hope and confidence in Him alone. I delight myself in the Lord, and He gives me the desires and secret petitions of my heart. The Lord withholds no good thing from me because I walk uprightly, following His commands and purposes for my life. My heavenly Father knows what I need before I even ask and generously supplies my every need according to His riches and glory in Christ Jesus. As I devote my heart and soul to seeking the Lord, my God, I will prosper in every way, even as my soul prospers.

When I honor the Lord with a tenth of my income, He opens the floodgates of heaven and pours out an abundance of blessing. It is my heart's desire to sow generously into the kingdom of God, so that blessings might come to others. As I do, I reap generously. God will provide and multiply my resources and increase the fruits of my righteousness—goodness, kindness and charity.

I thank You Father for Your blessings and favor, knowing that every good and perfect gift comes from You. I am content in my present circumstances and with what I have. I refuse to allow greed, lust and craving for earthly possessions to control my thoughts, for the love of money is the root of all evil. I trust in God, for He has promised that He will not fail me, give me up, nor leave me without support. I will not gather or store up for myself treasures on earth, for they will eventually perish. Instead, I will store up for myself treasures in heaven. For where my treasure is, my heart is also. I strive to do good works, and to be generous of heart, and ready to share with others. In this way, I am laying a firm foundation for the future, that I might grasp that which is life indeed.

(Jer.17:7; Psa.37:4; 84:11; Mat.6:8; Phi.4:19; 3Jo.1:2; Mal.3:10; 2Co.9:6-7; Jam.1:17; Heb.13:5; 1Ti.6:10; Mat.6:19-21; 1Ti.6:18-19; 2Co.9:10)

FORGIVENESS FOR OTHERS

I am a child of God, washed in His blood and totally forgiven as I walk in obedience to His will concerning forgiveness. With the grace of God and the strength of the Holy Spirit, I completely and repeatedly forgive those who sin against or inflict pain on someone I love or me. I totally release them from any and all responsibility for their wrongdoings regardless of their attitude, words or behavior toward me. I will allow Christ, my Mediator, to handle each case, not seeking revenge, but trusting Him to bring about justice and correction.

I am a light to the lost and a living testimony of Christ's mercy, love and willingness to forgive. I am not fretful or resentful, and I will not bear a grudge. I am quick to hear, slow to speak and slow to take offense or get angry, for this anger does not promote the righteousness God desires and requires of me. In obedience to God's Word, I erase any record of wrongs committed, believe and dwell only on the best in others, and, with the help of the Holy Spirit, discipline and control my thoughts and words.

By God's grace, no bitterness will spring forth in my soul. I purpose not to harbor hate in my heart and not to gossip, grumble, complain or slander others. Instead, I speak only words that edify and strengthen others as I concentrate solely on whatsoever things are true, positive, excellent and of good report. And finally, I lift up in prayer those who have wronged me or someone I love — interceding on their behalf and petitioning God's richest blessings on them.

(Mat.6:14-15; Rom.1:5; Luk.17:3-4; 1Pe.4:8; Pro.22:23; Rom.12:19; Acts13:47; 1Co.13:5; Lev.19:18; Jam.1:19-20; 1Co.13:7; Gal.5:22-23; Heb.12:15; Lev.19:16-17; Col.3:8; Phi.4:8; Mat.5:44; Luk6:28)

FORGIVENESS FOR SELF

I am happy and blessed because my sins are covered in the blood of Jesus. There is now no condemnation for me in Christ Jesus, because I walk not after the desires of my flesh, but by the leading of the Holy Spirit.

As I openly acknowledge and confess the sins of my past, Christ forgives me and takes away my guilt. I choose to leave my past at the foot of the cross and walk forward toward that which lies ahead, for I am a new creation; the old has passed away. God has clothed me with the garments of salvation and a robe of righteousness.

As God's chosen one, purified, holy, and well-loved by God, I clothe myself with compassion, kindness, humility, gentleness and patience — which have the power to endure.

I accept my forgiveness and remind

myself often that I am righteous in Christ Jesus, by the precious blood He shed on Calvary. His grace is enough for me in every situation. I do not chasten myself for being weak, for Christ's strength and power are shown effectively in my weakness. I am more than a conqueror and gain overwhelming victory through Him Who loves me.

I resist Satan's attempts to make me dislike myself or to walk in shame, guilt or discouragement. I take every thought captive into the obedience of Christ. God created me and knows that I am made of dust. He does not expect me to walk in perfection, but in love and obedience to His commands. I accept myself exactly as I am, assured that I was perfectly formed in my mother's womb by the hand of God and that He designed me with a specific purpose in mind. I praise God and celebrate the person God has ordained for me to be.

(Psa.32:1; Rom.8:1; Psa.32:5; Phi.3:13; 2Co.5:17;

Isa.61:10; Col.3:12; 2Co.5:21; 12:9; Rom.8:37; 2Co.10:5; Psa.103:14; 2Jo.1:6; Psa.139:13; Jer.29:11; Psa.139:16)

FORGIVENESS OF GOD

Praise be to the Lord Who is good and ready to forgive. He is abundant in mercy and loving-kindness to all those who call upon Him—showering them with His riches. Everyone who calls on the name of the Lord is saved. For God did not send His Son into the world to judge the world, but that the world might find salvation through Him.

I acknowledge and confess with out loud that Jesus is Lord and believe in my heart that God raised Him from the dead; therefore, I am saved. The Lord does not punish me after my sin because I reverently and worshipfully fear Him. For as the heavens are high above the earth, so great is His mercy and loving-kindness toward me. As far as the east is from the west, so far has He removed my transgressions from me. He blots them out, for His sake, and remembers them no more.

God is Light; there is no darkness in Him at all. I live and walk in the Light, just as He is in the Light, and the blood of Jesus Christ, His Son, cleanses me from all sin and guilt. He saved me, not because of any works of righteousness that I have done, but because of His own grace and mercy, by the cleansing of the new birth and renewing of the Holy Spirit which He poured out so richly upon me through Jesus Christ my Savior. He did this that I might be justified by His grace—His undeserved favor—and that I might become an heir of eternal life according to my hope in Him.

(Psa.86:5; Rom.10:12-13; Joh.3:17; Rom.10:9; Psa.103:10-12; Isa.43:25; 1Joh.1:5,7; Tit.3:4-7)

GENERATIONAL CURSES

God showed and clearly proved His love for me in that while I was yet a sinner, Christ died for me. I have been made righteous by the blood of Christ. I am saved and daily delivered from sin's dominion through His resurrection.

Because I receive, trust in and rely on His name, I no longer belong to or claim any earthly bloodline, but only that of the Spirit of God. I have been born again into an inheritance reserved in heaven for me, an imperishable inheritance which is beyond the reach of change and decay.

The Lord God visits the iniquity of the fathers upon the children to the third and fourth generation of those who hate Him and serve gods other than Him. I am totally and forever exempt from this curse because I am washed in the blood of Jesus. I am engrafted in Christ; I am a new creation—a new creature altogether.

The old has passed away, and the new has come!

Any curse, which was in force or stood against my family or me, has been forever cancelled and thoroughly blotted out. Christ set it aside and cleared me of it completely by nailing it to the cross. God disarmed the principalities and powers that rage against me and made a public example of them, triumphing over them in Christ and in the cross.

God acknowledges me as His own by putting His seal upon me and giving me His Holy Spirit in my heart as a guarantee of the fulfillment of His promise. God shows mercy and steadfast love to a thousand generations of those who love Him and keep His commandments. He is gracious, slow to anger and abundant in lovingkindness and truth, forgiving iniquity and transgression and sin. His faithfulness is from generation to generation. I am free from curses now and forevermore.

(Rom.5:8; Rom.5:10; Joh.1:13; 1Pe.1:4; Exo.20:3-5; 2Co. 5:17; Col.2:14-15; 2Co.1:22; Exo.20:6; 34:6-7; Psa.119:90)

GRATITUDE

Bless the Lord, O my soul, and all that is deep within me. Bless His holy name! I enter into His gates with thanksgiving! I greatly rejoice in my Lord; I praise the name of God with song and testify of His great works. My soul exults in God, for He has clothed me with the garments of salvation and covered me with the robe of righteousness. Jesus, You carry me in Your loving arms when I am weary and You bear my burdens. You intercede and intervene for me with the Father. You are the Light of my world. Because I follow You, I do not walk in darkness, but have the Light, which is Life. God has promised that He will never, in any way, fail me, give me up, nor leave me without support. I bless the Lord, for He is faithful and never changes.

My God, Who gave up His own Son for me, freely and graciously gives me all things. He supplies my every need according to His riches in glory in Christ Jesus. With all that is within me, I gratefully praise His Name as I remember all His benefits. He forgives my sins and never holds a grudge against me. He has redeemed my life from the pit and from corruption, heals all my diseases, and crowns me with loving-kindness and tender mercy. He satisfies my needs and desires with good things, executes righteousness and justice for me when I am oppressed, and has personally made known His ways to me. He is merciful, gracious and slow to anger.

I sing a new song to the Lord, for He has done marvelous things. I will cling tightly to God, for His mighty arm leads me. His strong right hand holds me, and He has promised to never relax His grip or let me go. In all things, God works for my good because I love Him and have been called according to His design and purpose.

With psalms, hymns and spiritual songs, I offer praise to God and make melody in my heart. I give thanks at all times and for everything in the name of my Lord, Jesus Christ, to God, my Father.

(Psa.103:1; 69:30-31; 100:4; Isa.61:10; Psa.68:19; Heb.7:25; Joh.8:12; Heb.13:5; Deu.7:9; Mal.3:6; Rom.8:32; Phi.4:19; Psa.103:2-10; Psa.98:1; 89:13; 63:8; Rom.8:28; Eph.5:19-20)

GUIDANCE

God has a plan and purpose for my life. He is acquainted with all my ways and leads me in the paths of righteousness for His name's sake. God has delivered and saved me. He leads me in a life of holiness by His grace and for His glory. I am confident in the Lord's leading and do not rely on my own insight or understanding. I acknowledge God in all my ways, and He directs my paths.

I do not submit to the advice of the ungodly, nor spend time in the company of sinners. Instead, I meditate constantly on the Word of God. I bear rich fruit like a tree planted by the water. Everything I do prospers.

The Holy Spirit guides me into the whole Truth, teaches me all things, and reminds me of all He has told me. I quiet my soul and rest in the assurance and confidence that the Lord's thoughts and ways are higher than my thoughts and ways. For God's way is perfect. The Word of the Lord is tested and tried. The Word is a lamp to my feet and a light to my path.

The Lord takes pleasure in me because I reverently and worshipfully fear Him and place my hope in His mercy and loving-kindness. My steps are directed and established by the Lord because He delights in my way. When I ask, God freely gives me wisdom. The Lord keeps His eye on me, counsels me and instructs me in the way that I should go, leading me along a clear and open path.

The Lord is my Rock and my Fortress, continually guiding me in rough places, keeping me from hidden danger, and making my crooked way straight. He goes before me to show me His path, beside me to accompany me, and behind me to protect me. He will never fail me nor let me go. I worship and exalt the majestic Name of the One Who keeps me from stumbling and presents me blameless, with joy and delight, to the one true God, through Jesus Christ, my Lord.

(Jer.29:11; Psa.139:3; 23:3; 2Ti.1:9; Pro.3:5-6; Psa.1:1-3; Joh.16:13; 14:26; Psa.37:7; Isa.55:9; 45:4; Psa.18:30; 119:105; 147:11; 37:23; Jam.1:5;Psa.32:8; Pro.4:11-12; Psa.31:3; Isa.58:11; Pro.3:26; Psa.139:5; Deu.31:8; Jud.1:24-25)

HEALING

Lord Jesus Christ, You were wounded for my transgressions, bruised for my guilt and by Your stripes–I am healed and made whole. I have died to sin and live to righteousness because of the Cross of Christ.

I confess my sins before you that they be forgiven and release the prayer of faith that will save me from my sickness, and I have confidence that Your loving Hand will restore me. I will obey Your command and ask the elders to anoint me with oil and have them pray with me for my healing.

Jesus, I know You have heard my prayer and forgiven all of my iniquities and healed me of all my diseases.

Father God, You sent Your Word to heal and rescue me from the grave. As I seek a right relationship with You, Your light breaks forth like the morning and brings forth in me restoration and the power of new life.

As I revere Your name, You will arise with healing in Your wings and I will go forth and leap with joy.

As I walk in the good news of the Gospel, I will be healed of every disease, weakness and infirmity. I am made whole by the power of Your Word. I will arise and go forth.

I release the faith that I have in You to heal me of all my diseases, for Your Word is life to those who find it and health to all our flesh.

Your favor surrounds me as a shield so I know that no weapon –or disease– formed against me will prevail for this is my inheritance as Your child. Anything that has not been planted by You shall be torn up by the roots.

I thank You, because what the enemy has hidden in darkness You have exposed and covered with Your precious Blood. The Blood of the Spotless Lamb is on the doorpost of my soul and the death angel cannot penetrate it.

You have come that I might have abundant life and Your grace and mercy sustains, refreshes and strengthens me in my time of suffering. Jesus, You are the Lord of my life and You have promised to bind my wounds and heal my afflictions. According to Your Word, You have taken my sin, disease and afflictions to the Cross; therefore, no disease has authority over my body.

Father God, You have set before me life and death. I choose life. You have set before me blessing and curses. I choose the blessing. Any generational curses that have tormented my family will be destroyed by the power of Your Word.

I reject any infirmity and every form of witchcraft and every type of warfare that has come against my body.

Lord, I thank You that through the sacrifice of Jesus on the Cross, I have passed out from under the curse and entered into the blessings of Abraham whom You blessed in all things —I am blessed with good health and favor.

I will not fear, for You are with me —You are my God. You promise to strengthen, help and uphold me with Your righteous Right Hand. When I hear Your voice and obey Your commandments none of the diseases of Egypt will come upon me for You are the Lord who heals me. You laid Your hands on the sick and they were healed.

I was bought with a price and I will glorify the Lord with my body for my body is a temple of the Holy Spirit. I am not my own. I will talk of Your wonderous works. I will give You thanks for You are good. I will declare Your greatness and bless Your name forever and ever.

(Psa. 105:2; 145:1, Isa. 41:10; 53:5; 54:17; 58:8 , Mal. 4:2, Mat. 4:23; 15:13, Acts 9:34; 14:9, Jam. 6:15, Ex.. 12:7, 13;15:26; Gal.3:13-14; 1 Cor. 6:19; Luke 4:40)

HEALTHY PREGNANCY

My child is a gift from the Lord; the fruit of my wife's womb—a reward. God secretly forms and intricately knits together my child's inward parts in the womb of my beloved.

As I diligently meditate on God's Word, He brings life and health to the child within my wife. I pray a hedge of protection around my child, assured that no weapon formed against my child shall prosper, for I am a servant of the Lord. According to God's Word, His angels, who have the full attention of God, guard and preserve the life of my child.

God knows the thoughts and plans He has for my child—thoughts and plans for my baby's welfare and peace, not for evil. Thoughts and plans to give my child hope for the future. All will go well with my child as I obey God's voice and do what is right in the sight of the Lord.

My baby is formed in the image of God and already holds, enjoys and benefits from God's richest blessings.

(Psa.127:3; 139:13; Pro.4:21-22; Job1:10; Isa.54:17; Psa.91:11; Mat.18:10; Jer.29:11; Deu.5:29; 12:25; Gen.1:27; Psa.147:13)

HOPE

I will be secure and confident because I have hope in You, O Lord. My hope will never leave me because You are with me. You made me hope, Father God, from the time I was at my mother's breast.

As I wait on you, I will be strong and my heart will have courage, for You have promised never to leave me nor forsake me.

Oh my God, I trust, rely and have hope in You! You promised never to disappoint me. Because of my hope in You, I will not be afraid. You have promised to provide for me and mine.

I hope in Your loving-kindness and mercy.
I only hope in You for You are my God.
I will hope in Your powerful Name for it
is good. I hope in You, for You are my
hiding place and my shield.

I waited and hoped on You, and You
brought to me my salvation! Because I
hope in You, O God, You will protect me
and give me peace of mind. Even though
You are not far from me, I will constantly
dwell in Your hope.

I rejoice in my hope for I will enjoy the
glory of God and my eternal salvation.
My hope in You will never leave—I hope
in those things that are not seen because
I trust and hope in You! Even when I
am suffering trouble I will hope in You!
Because of Your Word, I cherish my hope
in You.

As I abide in hope, I abide in You. Hope
endures everything. Your grace has come
and brought me salvation; Your Word has
trained me to lead a godly life as I look

and wait for the appearing of Jesus Christ my Savior—my Blessed Hope.

(1 Cor. 13:7,13;Titus 2:13; Rom. 5:2; 8:25; 12:12; 15:4; Isaiah 25:9; 26:3; Acts 17:27; Psalm 22:9; 25:2; 27:14; 32:7; 33:18; 42:5; 52:9; 71:14; Gen 50:21)

INFERTILITY

My God is able to do exceedingly, far over and above all that I dare to ask or think—infinitely beyond my highest prayers, desires, thoughts, hopes or dreams—according to His power that is at work within me.

I speak the Word of God over the womb of my bride because the Word of God is alive and full of power—active, operative, energizing and effective. This power of God is fully and completely available to me because I believe in the Lord, Jesus Christ. I claim and release this immeasurable and unlimited power over our lives, knowing, with full confidence that God is working in me. Because the same Spirit that raised Christ from the dead lives in me, He, Who raised Christ from the dead, also gives life to my mortal body through His Spirit, Who lives in me.

My God makes the barren woman a joyful mother of children. He has the power to open and shut wombs. Though Sarah's womb was dead, God promised her a son—an heir to the covenant promise He had made with Abraham. And the Lord visited Sarah and did for her as God had promised.

The Lord knows the desire of my heart for a child, and He promises to grant me the desires and secret petitions of my heart as I delight myself in Him. He opens His hand and satisfies me with gracious and merciful favor. He is near when I call to Him in sincerity and truth, and He fulfills my desires because I reverently and worshipfully fear Him.

As my father Abraham, I believe in God, Who gives life to the dead and calls into being that which does not exist. I hope, in faith, that God will grant the desire of my heart, open her womb, and place a child within. I will not weaken in faith when I consider a doctor's report.

Your Word says I am to deal with her barrenness with praise and worship so You can release Your miraculous provision upon her. No unbelief or distrust will cause me to waver concerning God's promise. Rather, I will grow strong and be empowered by faith as I give praise and glory to God, fully satisfied and assured that God is able and mighty to keep His Word and do all that He has promised.

(Eph.3:20; Heb.4:12; Eph.1:19; Rom.8:11; Gen.17:19; 21:1; Psa.37:4; 145:16-19; Rom.4:17-21; Isaiah 54:1)

MARRIAGE

I left my father and mother and was united, inseparably to my wife and we have become one flesh. What God has joined together no man can separate. I am head of our home as Christ is the Head of the church. I understand that my wife is subject to me and I am to love her as Christ loved the church, even unto death. I keep strife out of my life and out of my marriage so that there will not be confusion, disharmony, rebellion, and all sorts of evil and vile practices in our home and so that my prayers will be effective and not hindered.

The Love of God suffers long, is kind, does not envy or parade itself and is not puffed up; it does not behave rudely, does not seek its own way, is not provoked, thinks no evil; it does not rejoice in iniquity but in the truth; it bears all things, believes all things, endures all things. This is the kind of love I want in my marriage for this kind of love never fails and neither will my marriage!

(Mat. 19:5-6; Eph. 5:23-25; Jam. 3:16; 1 Pet. 3:7; 1 Cor. 13:4-8)

PARENTING

Jesus said, "Let the little children come to Me—for to such belongs the kingdom of God." And as they came, He took them, one by one, into His arms and blessed them. My children are a gift from God. I place them, daily, in His arms as I teach them to walk in His way. I will bless my children daily as Jesus blessed the little children.

Keeping their individual personalities and gifts in mind, I train my children in the way they should go and rejoice that they will not depart from it. With wisdom from God, I will compassionately discipline them because I love them, just as God disciplines me for my own good, that I might share in His holiness. I am careful not to let personal anger or resentment influence my judgment or actions as I strive to maintain the same attitude, purpose, and humble mind in me that is in Christ Jesus. Though discipline is painful and hard to bear at the time, it yields a peaceable fruit of righteousness in my children. As the rod and reproof give them wisdom, my children are a delight to my heart.

I deal with my children in kindness and rejoice with them when right and truth prevail. I believe the best about them and endure everything without weakening; my hope does not fade under any circumstances. Because I am God's chosen representative of Himself to my children, I clothe myself with tenderhearted grace and mercy, kindness, humility, gentleness and patience. I stand with my children when they fail, patiently encouraging them. I keep no record of their wrongs, but forgive them as Christ forgives me, blotting out and canceling their transgressions for Christ's sake. As they repent of their sins, I will strive for new beginnings and remember their sins no more.

I will teach and impress the Word of God

upon the hearts and minds of my children in order to thoroughly equip them for every good work, for all Scripture is God-inspired and useful for teaching rebuking, correcting and training in righteousness. I spend time with my children, reading the Word of God and singing spiritual songs of praise, making melody in my heart to the Lord. I laugh with them, for a happy heart is good medicine and a cheerful mind works healing.

I do not lose heart and grow weary, for in due time and at the appointed season, my children shall reap a harvest of righteousness. As God pours out His Spirit and blessings on my children, they will spring up among the grass like willows by the streams.

(Mar.10:13-16; Heb.2:13; Pro.22:6; Jam.1:5; Pro.13:24; Heb.12:10; Pro.19:18; Phi.2:5; Heb.12:11; Pro.29:15,17; 1Co.13:4-7; Col.3:12; Rom.15:1; 1Th.5:14; Lev.19:18; Mat.6:14; Col.2:14; Deu.6:7; 2Ti.3:16-17; Eph.5:19; Pro.17:22; Gal.6:9; Isa.44:3-4)

PRAISE

From the rising of the sun to its going down, I confess, praise and glorify Your name forevermore! I bow down and kneel in worship, entering into Your courts with praise and come before Your presence with singing, for You are good. Your work is honorable and glorious; Your righteousness endures forever.

I worship You Lord—for Your loving-kindness, truth and faithfulness; I magnify Your Word and Your name in all things! My lips pour forth praise, with thanksgiving and renewed trust, for the fulfillment of Your Word.

I lift up my hands in holiness, and bless You, the Lord, at all times with my whole heart; Your praise is continually in my mouth!

You are my Strength and my Shield. My heart confidently trusts in You, and I am empowered with faith as I offer praise and worship to Your Holy Name.

I will praise You, my God and King. I will bless Your Name every day and forevermore. Great is Your Name and You are greatly to be praised. Let everything that hath breath praise the Lord.

(Psa.113:3; 95:6; 100:2-4; 111:3; 138:2; 119:171, 103; 134:2; 86:12; 34:1; 21:13; 28:7; Rom.4:20; Psa. 145:1; 150:6)

PROTECTION

Lord, You are my protection. As a child of God, I live in Your presence. You go before me and behind me to hem me in, and Your hand is on me. I come to You and find refuge under Your wings. When I call on Your name, Jesus—You are near. You hear my cry and save me.

In times of danger, You are my shield. Your name is a strong tower—safe and high above evil. As I bring my petitions to You, with thanksgiving, the Father's peace surrounds my heart and mind.

When battles come my way, I am not

afraid or dismayed because the battles belong to God and He is with me. When the enemy comes in like a flood, the Spirit of the Lord lifts up a standard against him and puts him to flight. Lord, You are faithful. You strengthen me, set me on a firm foundation, and guard me from the evil one. You are my refuge and fortress! On You I lean and rely, and in You I confidently trust.

(Psa.41.12; 139:5; Rth.2:12; Psa.145:18-19; Pro.30:5; 18:10; Phi.4:7; 2Ch.20:17; Isa.59:19; 2Th:3; Psa.91:2)

RECONCILIATION

I was reconciled to God, the Father, by Your death at the cross. I have the peace of reconciliation so I may enjoy peace with God. All things are from God, who through Jesus Christ, reconciled me to Himself and gave to me the ministry of reconciliation, that by my words and my actions I strive to bring others into harmony with Him.

As Christ's ambassador I represent His love to bring reconciliation and peace to my family, friends and those You bring into my life.

Thank you Lord for reconciling me to the Father by Your blood.

(Rom. 5:1, 10; 2 Cor. 5:20; Col. 1:20)

RELATIONSHIPS . . . AS A SINGLE FATHER

Father, I have no wife and I place my children in Your loving arms to protect and nourish them as only You can. Your Word promises to bless them. You are their caregiver; You discipline them and they will yield to You and respect You. I thank You for the love, grace and mercy You bestow upon my children.

I know that You will give me the confidence and wisdom I need to lead them in the paths of righteousness. I will put

Your Word into my children and when they are old they will not depart from the paths You have chosen for them. I praise You because You are not only my Savior and Redeemer, You are also my nurturer, and You will take care of me as I take care of my children.

My children and I will want for nothing for You are our source. You will give us hands full of purpose, and Your favor will not depart from our lives.

I thank You and praise Your precious Name for You are good and Your loving kindness will partner with me to raise and provide for my children.

(Prov. 14:1)

RELATIONSHIPS . . .
AS A HUSBAND

I hold my marriage in honor and I esteem it to be worthy, precious and of great price. I have been joined inseparably to my wife, and we have become one flesh. God has designed me to be my wife's helpmate that she might not be alone.

I have authority over my wife and strive not to abuse this relationship, but to love my wife as Christ loved the Church and work to lead a godly life, knowing that it will draw her closer to the Lord. I conduct myself with humility, patience and a deep respect for my wife. I honor, appreciate, admire and praise her and am devoted and deeply in love with her.

As Christ is the authority in the Church, I am to be the authority and head of my household. I will dedicate myself to caring for my wife, being slow to anger and quick to praise her. Though she is to be subject to me I will never treat her as an inferior, for she is my helpmate and partner in all things. It is for me to build her up and edify her in all her endeavors. This is my proper duty in the Lord. My marriage bed remains undefiled, and I will not refuse or deprive my wife of her marital rights. We will devote ourselves to a specified time of unhindered prayer.

My wife is able to confidently trust and rely on me. As a man of God, I am clothed in strength, dignity and kindness, and give wise counsel and instruction. I will comfort, encourage and do my wife only good as long as there is life within me.

(Heb.13:4a; Mat.19:5; Gen.2:24; 1Pe.3:7; Eph.5:21-33; Col.3:19; Heb.13:4b; 1Co.7:5; Pro.18:22)

RELATIONSHIPS . . . AS FATHER OF A BLENDED FAMILY

As father of a blended family, I follow Christ's example and welcome each one of my children with open arms. I daily lift them up in prayer and bless them in the name of Jesus. I seek and receive wisdom from God to train them in the way they should go, so that when they grow older, they will not depart from it.

I accept my wife's children and my birth children as equals—not playing favorites in any way. O Lord search my heart to help me stay pure in this area. I have taken my wife's children in my heart just as God, in Christ, has taken me in His heart.

As I lead and support my wife and through her godly submission to me, I teach my children how to submit to God. As I love, respect and honor my wife, I teach my children how to love, respect and honor God. I will train and require my children to honor my wife and myself, for this is Your desire. My children will have long life and it will go well with them for God will bless them.

Jesus Christ is the head of our home. You have given our family a spirit of unity as we follow You. We are learning to accept one another just as Christ accepted us. You are our peace and You break down every wall of hostility. Each and every member of our family is important—crucial to our well-being and success. As my wife and I became one flesh when we were married, our family is one in Christ.

My children are learning about the goodness and faithfulness of God, so, together, with united hearts and one voice, our family may praise and glorify the God and Father of our Lord Jesus Christ.

(Mar.10:16; Jam.1:5; Pro.22:6; Jam.2:1; Psa.139:23-24; Joh.1:12; Eph.5:22-23; Deu.5:16; Col.3:20; Rom.15:5,7; Eph.2:14; 1Co.12:12; Rom.12:4-5; 15:6)

RELATIONSHIPS . . . AS A WIDOWER

Father, You are the Lord of Hosts, my Maker and my nurturer. You nourish, protect and cherish me, even as You do the Church. You execute justice on my behalf. You promise that my state as a widower will not bring me prolonged grieving because my Maker is my nuturer. You uphold me, set me upright and secure my boundaries.

I fix my hope in You. You have comforted me during my time of loss. You hold me during my grief and give me hope for tomorrow. I will not worry about my future for You promised the righteous will not be forsaken. I cry out and You hear me. I will rest in You for Your banner over me is Love.

(Isa. 54:5,6; Eph.5:29; Psa. 34:17; 37:7,25)

RELEASING THE WORD IN MY LIFE

In the name of Jesus, I come to God in prayer to repent of my ignorance of the Word of God and to ask Him to forgive me for the foolish things I have prayed.

I bind every word from my mouth that has released the devil or drawn his weapons toward me, in the name of Jesus. I bind every hindering force that I've ever given strength to by the words of my mouth, and I break the power of those spiritual forces in Jesus' name.

I ask for and receive wisdom and understanding from God to set in motion, through scriptural methods, all that is good, pure, perfect, lovely and of good report.

I covenant with God to pray accurately. I will keep guard over my mouth and speak only that which glorifies God. I will let no corrupt communication proceed from my mouth, but only that which edifies and ministers grace to the hearer. I will not grieve the Holy Spirit of God, whereby I am sealed to the day of Redemption, but will give glory and honor and praise to the Lord Jesus Christ for all that has been and shall be done.

I thank my heavenly Father that I am the Body of Christ. The enemy has no power over me. I proclaim that all that is good, all that is blessed of God, all that is in the perfect will of God, and all that God has designed for me shall come to me, in Jesus' name.

All the evil, all the bad reports, and all that the enemy has designed to deceive me, to lead me astray, and to destroy my home, my finances or me shall be stopped with the name of Jesus and the words of my mouth.

I'm blessed in the city and blessed in the field. I'm blessed in the baskets and blessed in the store. I'm blessed coming in and going out. I'm the head and not the tail. I'm above and not beneath. I'm blessed of almighty God, strengthened with all might according to His glorious power. The Greater One is in me; He puts me over in life. The Spirit of Truth is in me; He gives me divine wisdom, direction, and understanding of every situation and every circumstance of life. I have the wisdom of God and the mind of Christ, and I thank my heavenly Father for His Spirit, Who leads me. In Jesus' name.

(2Ti.2:15; Jam.4:3; Ecc.5:2; Pro.6:2; Mat.12:37; Luk.10:19; Mat.6:6-7; Eph.5:4; Heb.10:24-25; Eph.4:30; Psa.150:2; 111:2-3; Rom.12:5; Col.2:15; Psa.84:11-12; 138:7; Rev.12:11; Deu.28:3-13; 2Co.12:9; 1Jo.4:4; Joh.14:17; 2Ti.1:14; 1Jo.2:27; 1Co.2:15-16; Psa.32:8)

RESTORATION

You have taken away my stony heart and given me a heart of flesh. You have given me a new heart and put a new spirit within me. Your light shines forth in me like the morning. My restoration and the power of new life springs forth quickly. My righteousness in God goes before me, and the glory of the Lord is my rear guard.

I am daily delivered from sin's dominion through Your resurrected life. I have been crucified with Christ, and it is no longer I who live, but Christ living in me. The life I now live in the body I live by complete trust in and reliance on the Son of God, Who loves me and gave Himself up for me.

There is no condemnation for me in Christ. I do not conform myself to this world, but am transformed by the entire renewing of my mind so that I can prove the acceptable and perfect will of God for me.

God restores for me the years the locusts have eaten. I praise the name of the Lord, Who deals wondrously with me. I know, understand and realize that God is with me and that He is the Lord, my God, and there is none like Him. And He Who began a good work in me will continue until Christ returns—developing, perfecting and bringing the good work to full completion in me.

(Gal. 2:20; 3:26; Rom. 8:1; 12:2; Joel 2:25-26; Phil 1:6, 20; Ps. 23:3; 80:3; Eze.36:26, Isa. 58:8)

SERVANTHOOD

I serve the Lord with gladness, for I am His handiwork, recreated in Christ Jesus, to do the good works He has planned for me to do. I want to serve You, Lord, with passion. As I allow God's Light to shine through my good deeds, my God will be glorified.

In both service and spiritual worship, I dedicate my body as a living sacrifice—holy, devoted and well pleasing to God.

I work heartily at every task, for I am actually serving the Lord when I minister to others. In kindness and mercy, I do justice to the weak, poor and fatherless.

With love in my heart, I submit my time, talents and energy to be used by God in ministering to the needs of others, according to His leading.

God sends favor and blessing to me, providing all that I need to finish every good work in abundance. I cling to God, conforming wholly to His example, as I serve others in His name. When I am tired and tempted to lose heart, I will come close to You, Lord Jesus, and You will renew my strength. You enable me to run without growing weary and walk without becoming faint.

I thank God for giving me the strength and ability to serve others, for judging me and counting me faithful and trustworthy, and for appointing me to this ministry. I arm myself with the Word of God, that I might be equipped for every good work. I set myself apart from corrupt and unclean influences. Thus, I am a useful vessel–consecrated and profitable to the

Master, fit and ready to fulfill His will and purpose.

(Psa.100:2; Eph.2:10; Mat.5:14-16; Rom.12:1; Col.3:23-24; Pro.14:21; Gal.5:13; Rom.12:13; 2Co.1:4;9:8; Joh.12:26; Gal.6:9; Isa.40:31; 1Ti.1:12; 2Ti. 2:21)

SPIRIT OF JOY

I leap for joy because my name is recorded in heaven and my abundant reward waits for me there. I rejoice in God's deliverance; my inner being is filled with gladness because He has redeemed me. I am called by His name, and His Word brings rejoicing to my heart!

I am a child of God, forgiven and set free from sin. The Holy Spirit is working in my soul; therefore, the spiritual fruit of joy operates freely in my life. God adds to my joy because I walk in meekness and conduct myself in a manner worthy and fully pleasing to the Lord, bearing fruit in every good work and steadily growing in the knowledge of God. As I delight in righteousness, God anoints my head with the oil of triumphant joy and gladness, for the kingdom of God is righteousness and peace and joy in the Holy Spirit.

The joy of the Lord is my strength. It fills my heart as I walk in His Light, His favor and His protection. I sing for joy because the Lord comforts me and shows me compassion. I shout for joy because He makes a covering over me and defends me.

I rejoice in You my God. You are my strength, my song and my salvation; You fill me with joy and gladness. How great is the goodness of God for me because I fear, revere and worship Him. Because I trust and take refuge in Him, He hides me in the secret place of His presence where there is fullness of joy.

(Luk.6:23; 10:20; Psa.35:9; 71:23; Jer.15:16; Acts 2:38; Gal.5:22; Isa.29:19; Ecc.2:26; Col.1:10; Heb.1:9; Neh.8:10; Psa.97:11; Isa.49:13; Psa.5:11; Isa.12:2; Psa.21:6)

SPIRITUAL WARFARE

I am the righteousness of Christ. No evil can harm me, for God has given me authority to overcome the power of the enemy. I will not fear because God is with me. I will not be dismayed because He is my God. He strengthens me, helps me and holds me with His victorious right hand of righteousness and justice. As a servant of God, I have inherited peace, righteousness, security and triumph over opposition. No weapon formed against me shall prosper. I overcome the enemy by the blood of the Lamb and the word of my testimony.

Satan comes to steal, kill and destroy, but Christ came that I might have and enjoy abundant life. The devil roams around like a lion roaring in fierce hunger, seeking to seize and devour me, but I withstand the enemy and remain firm in my faith. With God, I gain the victory. He tramples down my enemies.

There is no trial or temptation that comes to me that I cannot bear. God is faithful to His Word and His compassionate nature. He will not allow me to be tempted beyond my strength to resist or my power to endure.

The weapons of my warfare are not physical—of flesh and blood. Rather, they are mighty before God for the overthrow and destruction of strongholds. When the enemy comes against me, I cry out to God, Who is my shelter and my refuge, a strong tower against my adversary. You are always near to me, a very present help in trouble. You hear my cry and save me.

I count it all joy when trials and tribulations come my way, for the testing of my faith will produce patience. I will stand the test and will be approved; I will receive the victor's crown of life, which God has promised to those who love Him. Thanks be to God, Who makes me a conqueror and gives me victory in Christ Jesus!

(Luk.10:19; Isa.41:10; 54:17; Rev.12:11; Joh.10:10; 1Pe.5:8; Psa.60:12; 1Co.10:13; 2Co.10:4; Psa.61:3; 46:1; 145:18-19; Jam.1:12; 1Pe.5:9-10; 1Co.15:57)

SUBMISSION

I submit myself reverently and completely to God, offering my life as a living sacrifice to Him. I submit to and endure His discipline as it enables me to share in His holiness. In obedience to God's Word, I submit myself to every human institution and authority for His sake. I honor and respect my parents, for this is pleasing to God.

I will learn Your Word in silence with all submission. As I submit to God and resist Satan, he must flee from me. I will trust in Your mercy, and my heart will rejoice in Your salvation as I submit to You and Your loving kindness.

I obey and submit to my spiritual leaders and do my part to help them do their job with gladness. I am subject to those in authority over me in my workplace. I do my best with all my heart, out of reverence for the Lord and as a sincere expression of my devotion to Him.

In all my ways, with kindly affection, I give precedence and show honor to others.

I have the same attitude, purpose and humble mind in me that is in Christ Jesus. He is my example in humility. I am respectful, self-controlled and trustworthy in all things. All the words of my mouth are righteous, pure and pleasing to God.

I commit and trust all my works to God as I submit with the same mindset as Christ Jesus.

(2 Co.5:7; Pro.3:5-6; Phi.2:5; Pro.8:8; 15:26; Heb.12:7,10; 1Pe.2:13; Col.3:20; Heb.13:17; Col.3:22; Rom.12:10; Heb 11:6; 1Ti 2:11, Jam. 4:7; 2 Co. 5:7)

WAITING FOR A SPOUSE

As I delight myself in the Lord, He will give me the desire and secret petition of my heart for a wife and a helpmate. As I commit my way to God, trusting and relying only on Him, He will bring it to pass.

I am confident that when I make any request according to God's will, He listens and hears me. I know, with absolute knowledge, that He will grant my request. Therefore, I pray, according to His will for the woman who will one day be my wife. She will be a righteous woman of God, who will leave her mother and father and be joined to me as one flesh. I will love her as Christ loves the Church, nurturing and cherishing her forever. And what God joins together, man will not be able to separate.

I am not anxious for the future, but take one day at a time. As I commit myself to

God, lean on Him and confidently place my hope in Him, He keeps me in perfect and constant peace. With thanksgiving, I come to God with my specific request for a wife, as His peace guards my heart and mind in Christ Jesus.

The Lord knows the thoughts and plans He has for me—thoughts and plans for my welfare and peace, not for evil. Thoughts and plans to give me hope for my future. Your Word says none shall lack their mate; therefore, I will not lack mine. As I place my faith in God, He fills me with joy and peace, and, by the power of the Holy Spirit, causes my heart to bubble over with hope as I await my wife.

(Psa.37:4-5; 1Jo.5:14-15; 2Co.6:14; Eph.5:31,25,29; Mat.19:6; 6:34; Isa.26:3; 34:16; Phi.4:6-7; Jer.29:11; Rom.15:13)

WALKING IN FAITH

I am a man of God, declared righteous, through faith in Jesus Christ. I confidently and safely walk in the grace and favor of God—all His blessings are on my life and I am freely welcomed into His presence.

I belong to Christ and am, therefore, Abraham's offspring—an heir according to promise. I have been crucified with Christ; it is no longer I who live, but Christ Who lives in me. The life I now live in the body I live by faith in God, Who loved me and gave Himself up for me.

I walk by faith, not by sight or appearance. I trust in the Lord with all my heart and mind and do not rely on my own insight or understanding. In all my ways, I know and acknowledge Him, and He directs my paths.

I shut out distractions, focusing my love

and attention on Jesus, my Redeemer and Completer of my faith. My faith increases as I saturate myself in the Word of God and continually listen to your message, Lord.

I pursue faith, love, peace and righteousness—conforming to the will of God in thought, word and deed. As I walk in faith, I spend time in earnest prayer for nothing is impossible with God. My faith assures me of the things I hope for; it is the proof of things I cannot yet see. I pray with faith, believing and trusting, and when I ask, I will receive. When I seek, I find. And when I knock, the door is opened to me.

I build myself up, praying in the Holy Spirit. I guard and keep myself in the love of God as I expect and patiently wait for the mercy of my Lord, Jesus Christ, which will bring me into life eternal. And He Who began a good work in me will continue until the day of Christ's return.

I will walk in faith–for without faith it is impossible to please God. As I come to God and abide in Him in faith, I believe that He is real and faithful and rewards those who seek Him!

By faith I will obey God –

By faith I will receive strength –

By faith I will give praise to the King of Kings and Lord of Lords!

(Gal.3:29; Gal.2:20; 2Co.5:7; Pro.3:5-6; Eph.1:17; Rom.10:17; 2Ti.2:22; Pro.8:8; 15:26; Psa.34:14; Luk.1:37; Heb.11:1; Mat.21:22; Mar.11:24; Luk.11:10; 1Jo.5:15; Jud 1:20-21; Phi.1:6; Heb 11:6; 8:11, I Cor 7:35)

WISDOM

My life is blessed because I walk in the skillful wisdom of God, which He has stored away for the righteous. Because I continuously seek wisdom, I understand the reverent and worshipful fear of the Lord and find the knowledge of my God. When I find wisdom, I find life and receive favor from the Lord. Wisdom comes from God, and He gives it to me freely when I ask for it. I call on Him, and He answers me and shows me great and mighty things that I do not know. Your wisdom, Lord, is more precious than rubies and better than fine gold and nothing I desire can compare with it.

The wisdom of God brings me great blessings. It brings me long life, riches, honor and peace. God's wisdom is a tree of life and I cling to it! As I walk in wisdom, it keeps, defends and protects me. Because I love wisdom, it guards me. Wisdom brings honor and it promotes me.

By the grace of God and the wisdom He has given me, my character is pure, peace-loving, considerate and gentle. I am willing to yield to reason. I am full of compassion and good fruits. My thoughts and words are sincere, straightforward, impartial and free from doubt. I delight in Your wisdom Lord.

(Pro.3:13; 2:4-7; 8:35; Jam.1:5; Jer.33:3; Pro.3:14-15; 3:16-18; 4:6,8; Jam.3:17; Pro.7:4)

WORKPLACE

I am God's handiwork, created to do good works and walk in the paths He has prepared for me. I am ready and equal for any task through Christ, Who fills me with inner strength. He is my sufficiency. The Lord encourages my heart and strengthens me in every good work and word. God furnishes me with favor and earthly blessing at all times and in all things so that I accomplish the good works He sets before me. Whatever I do, whether in word or deed, I do it with all my might, in the name of the Lord Jesus, giving praise to God the Father.

I obey my employer and those I serve, showing respect and concern to please them. I work diligently, with all my heart, not to please man, but as if doing service to Christ Himself. For, whatever good I do, I receive my reward from the Lord. I am submissive and pleasing in my workplace. I prove myself to be loyal, faithful and entirely reliable so that I might do credit to the teachings of God, my Savior. My faithfulness refreshes the life of my employers and those I serve.

As I commit and trust my work and plans wholly to God, He causes my thoughts to become agreeable to His will and blesses the work of my hands with success. He illuminates my integrity and my righteousness in Christ, so that they shine like the noonday sun. I make it my ambition to live quietly and peacefully, to mind my own affairs, and to work with my hands. In this way, I command the respect of the outside world. I do all things without murmuring, faultfinding, complaining, questioning or doubting. In this way, I show myself as an honest and pure child of God. I am seen among those I work with as a bright light shining in a dark world.

I do not lose heart in doing right, for in due time I will reap a harvest. The everlasting God, the Lord, the Creator of the ends of the earth, fills me with power and strength when I am weak and tired. As I place my hope in Him, I run and do not grow weary. I walk and do not faint. When my ways please the Lord, He makes even my enemies at peace with me.

The work of my hands comes back to me as profit, and I receive honor for my patient and faithful obedience to all I serve. I enjoy the fruit of my labor, for it is a gift from God.

(Eph.2:10; Phi.4:13; 2Th.2:16-17; 2Co.9:8; Ecc.9:10; Col.3:17; Eph.6:5-8; Tit.2:9-10; Pro.25:13; 16:3; Psa.37:5-6; 1Th.4:11-12; Phi.2:14-15; Gal.6:9; Isa.40:28-31; Pro.16:7; 12:14; 14:23; 27:18; Ecc.3:13)

WORSHIP

Holy, Holy, Holy is the Lord God Almighty, Who was and Who is and Who is to come. The whole earth is full of His glory. I give Him the glory due His name and worship Him in the beauty of His Holiness. I bow down and kneel before You, Lord, for You are my God and I am the sheep of Your hand. You are my Shepherd and my Redeemer.

You are my High Priest, Who has paid the price for my sins and cleansed me from all unrighteousness that I might stand before God, shameless and without fear.

I worship God in spirit and in truth, for He is worthy to receive glory and honor. Worthy is the Lamb, Who was sacrificed for my salvation. All power, riches, wisdom, might, honor, majesty and blessing belong to Him! I lift up holy hands. To Him Who is seated on the throne and to the Lamb be glory forever and ever!

I will bless the name of the Lord at all times! His praise shall continually be in my mouth. With a loud voice, together with the angels in heaven, I will sing of the mercy and loving-kindness of the Lord forever. With my mouth will I make known His faithfulness to all generations!

(Rev.4:8; Isa.6:3; Psa.29:2; 95:6-7; Heb. 3:1; Eph.3:12; Joh.4:24; Rev.4:11; 5:12; 1Ti. 2:8; Psa.34:1; Rev.7:10; Psa.89:1)

Scripture Verses

Addictions

Rom. 6:17 But thank God, though you were once slaves of sin, you have become obedient with all your heart to the standard of teaching in which you were instructed and to which you were committed.

Rom. 6:18 And having been set free from sin, you have become the servants of righteousness (of conformity to the divine will in thought, purpose, and action).

Ps. 107:8 Oh, that Men would give thanks to the Lord for His goodness, and for His wonderful works to the children of Israel

Ps. 107:9 For He satisfies the longing soul and fills the hungry soul with good.

Ps. 107:10 Some sat in darkness and in the shadow of death, being bound in affliction and in irons

Ps. 107:11 Because they had rebelled against the words of God and spurned the counsel of the Most High.

Ps. 107:12 Therefore He bowed down their hearts with hard labor; they stumbled and fell down, and there was none to help.

Ps. 107:13 Then they cried to the Lord in their trouble, and He saved them out of their distresses.

Ps. 107:14 He brought them out of darkness and the shadow of death and broke apart the bonds that held them.

Ps. 107:20 He sends forth His word and heals them and rescues them from the pit and destruction.

2 Cor. 5:17 Therefore if anyone is in Christ, he is a new creation; old things have passed away; behold, all things have become new

Rom. 6:6 Knowing this, that our old man was crucified with Him, that the body of sin might be done away with, that we should no longer be slaves of sin

Rom. 6:7 For he who has died has been freed from sin

Gal. 2:20 I have been crucified with Christ, it is no longer I who live, but Christ lives in me and the life which I now live in the flesh I live by faith in the Son of God, Who loved me and gave Himself for me.

John 8:31 Then Jesus said to those Jews who believed Him, "If you abide in My word, you are My disciples indeed."

John 8:32 And you will know the Truth, and the Truth will set you free.

Titus 2:11 For the grace of God that brings salvation has appeared to all men

Titus 2:12 teaching us that, denying ungodliness and worldly lusts, we should live soberly righteously and godly in the present age.

Phil. 4:19 And my God will liberally supply your every need according to His riches in glory in Christ Jesus.

1 John 4:4 Little children, you are of God and have defeated and overcome them because He Who lives in you is greater than he who is in the world.

James 4:7 So be subject to God. Resist the devil, and he will flee from you.

James 4:8 Come close to God and He will come close to you. [Recognize that you are] sinners, get your soiled hands clean; wavering individuals with divided interests, and purify your hearts.

Phil. 4:13 I have strength for all things in Christ Who empowers me

Rom. 6:12 Let not sin therefore rule as king in your mortal bodies, to make you yield to its cravings and be subject to its lusts and evil passions.

Rom. 6:13 And do not present your members as instruments of unrighteousness to sin, but present yourselves to God as being alive from the dead, and your
members as instruments of righteousness to God.

Rom. 6:17 But thank God, though you were once
slaves of sin, you have become obedient with all your
heart to the standard of teaching in which you were
instructed and to which you were committed.

Rom. 6:18 And having been set free from sin, you have
become the servants of righteousness.

1 John 5:4 For whatever is born of God is victorious
over the world; and this is the victory that conquers
the world, even our faith.

1 John 5:5 Who is it that is victorious over the world
but he who believes that Jesus is the Son of God?

1 Peter 2:11 Beloved, I implore you as aliens and strang-
ers and exiles [in this world] to abstain from the
sensual urges that wage war against the soul.

Eph. 4:22 Strip yourselves of your former nature
which characterized your previous manner of life
and becomes corrupt through lusts and desires that
spring from delusion;

Rom. 8:5 For those who are according to the flesh and
are controlled by its unholy desires set their minds
on and pursue those things which gratify the flesh,
but those who are according to the Spirit and are
controlled by the desires of the Spirit set their minds
on and seek those things which gratify the [Holy]
Spirit.

1 John 2:16 For all that is in the world—the lust of the
flesh and the lust of the eyes and the pride of life
—these do not come from the Father but are from
the world.

Eph. 4:24 And put on the new nature created in God's
image, in true righteousness and holiness.

Col. 3:10 And have clothed yourselves with the new, which is renewed and remolded into knowledge after the image of Him Who created it.

Rom. 8:5 For those who are according to the flesh and are controlled by its unholy desires set their minds on and pursue those things which gratify the flesh, but those who are according to the Spirit and are controlled by the desires of the Spirit set their minds on and seek those things which gratify the [Holy] Spirit.

Rom. 8:9 But you are not living the life of the flesh, you are living the life of the Spirit, if the [Holy] Spirit of God dwells within you [directs and controls you]. But if anyone does not possess the [Holy] Spirit of Christ, he is none of His. [Rom. 8:14.]

Gal. 5:22 But the fruit of the [Holy] Spirit is love, joy, peace, patience, kindness, goodness, faithfulness,

Gal. 5:23 Gentleness, self-control. Against such things there is no law.

John 10:10 The thief comes only in order to steal and kill and destroy. I came that they may have and enjoy life, and have it in abundance.

Acts 20:32 And now, I commit you to God. And I commend you to the Word of His grace. It is able to build you up and to give you inheritance among all God's set-apart ones.

Ps. 119:11 Your word have I laid up in my heart, that I might not sin against You.

1 Peter 5:8 Be well balanced, be vigilant and cautious at all times; for that enemy of yours, the devil, roams around like a lion roaring, seeking someone to seize upon and devour.

Heb. 2:17 So it is evident that it was essential that He be made like His brethren in every respect, in order that He might become a merciful and faithful High Priest in the things related to God, to make atonement and propitiation for the people's sins.

Heb. 2:18 For because He Himself [in His humanity] has suffered in being tempted, He is able to run to the cry of those who are being tempted and tested and tried [and who therefore are being exposed to suffering].

2 Peter 2:9 Now if [all these things are true, then be sure] the Lord knows how to rescue the godly out of temptations and trials, and how to keep the ungodly under chastisement until the day of judgment and doom,

Heb. 4:16 Let us then fearlessly and confidently and boldly draw near to the throne of grace, that we may receive mercy [for our failures] and find grace to help in good time for every need.

Is. 41:10 Fear not, for I am with you; do not look around you in terror and be dismayed, for I am your God. I will strengthen and harden you to difficulties, yes, I will help you; yes, I will hold you up and retain you with My [victorious] right hand of rightness and justice. [Acts 18:10.]

Is. 42:16 And I will bring the blind by a way that they know not; I will lead them in paths that they have not known. I will make darkness into light before them and make uneven places into a plain. These things I have determined to do [for them]; and I will not leave them forsaken.

John 15:7 If you live in Me [abide vitally united to Me] and My words remain in you and continue to live in your hearts, ask whatever you will, and it shall be done for you.

Job 1:9 Then Satan answered the Lord, Does Job [reverently] fear God for nothing?

Job 1:10 Have You not put a hedge about him and his house and all that he has, on every side? You have conferred prosperity and happiness upon him in the work of his hands, and his possessions have increased in the land.

Deut. 33:27 The eternal God is your refuge and dwelling place, and underneath are the everlasting arms; He drove the enemy before you and thrust them out, saying, Destroy!

Ps. 23:4 Yes, though I walk through the valley of the shadow of death, I will fear or dread no evil, for You are with me; Your rod [to protect] and Your staff [to guide], they comfort me.

Ps. 138:7 Though I walk in the midst of trouble, You will revive me; You will stretch forth Your hand against the wrath of my enemies, and Your right hand will save me.

Rom. 12:21 Do not let yourself be overcome by evil, but overcome evil with good.

1 Thess. 5:21 But test and prove all things [until you can recognize] what is good; [to that] hold fast.

Rom. 12:2 And do not be conformed to this world, but be transformed by the renewing of your mind, that you may prove what is that good and acceptable and perfect will of God

Gal. 5:1 Stand fast therefore in the liberty by which Christ has made us free, and do not be entangled again with a yoke of bondage

Authority

1 Tim. 2:1 FIRST OF all, then, I admonish and urge that petitions, prayers, intercessions, and thanksgivings be offered on behalf of all men,

1 Tim. 2:2 For kings and all who are in positions of authority or high responsibility, that [outwardly] we may pass a quiet and undisturbed life [and inwardly] a peaceable one in all godliness and reverence and seriousness in every way.

1 Tim. 2:3 For such [praying] is good and right, and [it is] pleasing and acceptable to God our Savior,

1 Tim. 2:4 Who wishes all men to be saved and [increasingly] to perceive and recognize and discern and know precisely and correctly the [divine] Truth.

Ps. 143:10 Teach me to do Your will, for You are my God; let Your good Spirit lead me into a level country and into the land of uprightness.

Prov. 14:34 Uprightness and right standing with God [moral and spiritual rectitude in every area and relation] elevate a nation, but sin is a reproach to any people.

Heb. 13:18 Keep praying for us, for we are convinced that we have a good conscience, that we want to walk uprightly and live a noble life, acting honorably and in complete honesty in all things.

Heb. 4:12 For the Word that God speaks is alive and full of power; it is sharper than any two-edged sword, penetrating to the dividing line of the breath of life and [the immortal] spirit, and of joints and marrow, exposing and sifting and analyzing and judging the very thoughts and purposes of the heart.

Is. 55:1 WAIT and listen, everyone who is thirsty! Come to the waters; and he who has no money, come, buy and eat! Yes, come, buy wine and milk without money and without price.

Rom. 13:1 LET EVERY person be loyally subject to the governing authorities. For there is no authority except from God and those that exist do so by God's appointment. [Prov. 8:15.]

Col. 2:10 And you are in Him, made full and having come to fullness of life. And He is the Head of all rule and authority.

Rom. 13:3 For civil authorities are not a terror to [people of] good conduct, but to [those of] bad behavior. Would you have no dread of him who is in authority? Then do what is right and you will receive his approval and commendation.

Rom. 13:4 For he is God's servant for your good. But if you do wrong, be afraid, for he does not bear and wear the sword for nothing. He is God's servant to execute His wrath on the wrongdoer.

Titus 2:9 [Tell] bond servants to be submissive to their masters, to be pleasing and give satisfaction in every way. [Warn them] not to talk back or contradict,

Titus 2:10 Nor to steal by taking things of small value, but to prove themselves truly loyal and entirely reliable and faithful throughout, so that in everything they may be an ornament and do credit to the teaching [which is] from and about God our Savior.

1 Peter 2:13 Be submissive to every human institution and authority for the sake of the Lord, whether it be to the emperor as supreme,

1 Peter 2:17 Show respect for all men. Love the brotherhood. Reverence God. Honor the emperor.

1 Peter 2:18 Household servants, be submissive to your masters with all respect, not only to those who are kind and considerate and reasonable, but also to those who are surly.

Matt. 10:18 And you will be brought before governors and kings for My sake, as a witness to bear testimony before them and to the Gentiles (the nations).

Matt. 10:19 But when they deliver you up, do not be anxious about how or what you are to speak; for what you are to say will be given you in that very hour and moment,

Matt. 10:20 For it is not you who are speaking, but the Spirit of your Father speaking through you.

Matt. 5:14 You are the light of the world. A city set on a hill cannot be hidden.

Matt. 5:16 Let your light so shine before men that they may see your moral excellence and your praiseworthy, noble, and good deeds and recognize and honor and praise and glorify your Father Who is in heaven.

2 Chr. 7:14 If My people, who are called by My name, shall humble themselves, pray, seek, crave, and require of necessity My face and turn from their wicked ways, then will I hear from heaven, forgive their sin, and heal their land.

Blessings, Spiritual

Ps. 32:1 [A Psalm of David.] A skillful song, or a didactic or reflective poem. BLESSED is he who has forgiveness of his transgression continually exercised upon him, whose sin is covered.

Ps. 119:2 Blessed are they who keep His testimonies, and who seek, inquire for and of Him and crave Him with the whole heart.

John 1:16 For out of His fullness we have all received one grace after another and spiritual blessing upon spiritual blessing and even favor upon favor and gift upon gift.

Ezek. 34:26 And I will make them and the places round about My hill a blessing, and I will cause the showers to come down in their season; there shall be showers of blessing.

Gal. 3:14 To the end that through Christ Jesus, the blessing to Abraham might come upon the Gentiles, so that we through faith might receive the promise of the [Holy] Spirit.

Eph. 1:3 May blessing be to the God and Father of our Lord Jesus Christ Who has blessed us in Christ with every spiritual blessing in the heavenly realm!

Blessings, Material

Deut. 7:12 And if you hearken to these precepts and keep and do them, the Lord your God will keep with you the covenant and the steadfast love which He swore to your fathers.

Deut. 7:13 And He will love you, bless you, and multiply you; He will also bless the fruit of your body and the fruit of your land, your grain, your new wine, and your oil, the increase of your cattle and the young of your flock in the land which He swore to your fathers to give you.

Deut. 7:14 You shall be blessed above all peoples; there shall not be male or female barren among you, or among your cattle.

Deut. 28:1 IF YOU will listen diligently to the voice of the Lord your God, being watchful to do all His commandments which I command you this day, the Lord your God will set you high above all the nations of the earth.

Deut. 28:2 And all these blessings shall come upon you and overtake you if you heed the voice of the Lord your God.

Deut. 28:3 Blessed shall you be in the city and blessed shall you be in the field.

Deut. 28:4 Blessed shall be the fruit of your body and the fruit of your ground and the fruit of your beasts, the increase of your cattle and the young of your flock.

Deut. 28:5 Blessed shall be your basket and your kneading trough.

Deut. 28:6 Blessed shall you be when you come in and blessed shall you be when you go out.

Deut. 28:7 The Lord shall cause your enemies who rise up against you to be defeated before your face; they shall come out against you one way and flee before you seven ways.

Deut. 28:8 The Lord shall command the blessing upon you in your storehouse and in all that you undertake. And He will bless you in the land which the Lord your God gives you.

Deut. 28:9 The Lord will establish you as a people holy to Himself, as He has sworn to you, if you keep the commandments of the Lord your God and walk in His ways.

Deut. 28:10 And all people of the earth shall see that you are called by the name the Lord, and they shall be afraid of you.

Deut. 28:11 And the Lord shall make you have a surplus of prosperity, through the fruit of your body, of your livestock, and of your ground, in the land which the Lord swore to your fathers to give you.

Deut. 28:12 The Lord shall open to you His good treasury, the heavens, to give the rain of your land in its season and to bless all the work of your hands; and you shall lend to many nations, but you shall not borrow.

Deut. 28:13 And the Lord shall make you the head, and not the tail; and you shall be above only, and you shall not be beneath, if you heed the commandments of the Lord your God which I command you this day and are watchful to do them.

Ps. 67:6 The earth has yielded its harvest; God, even our own God, will bless us.

Gal. 3:14 To the end that through Christ Jesus, the blessing to Abraham might come upon the Gentiles, so that we through faith might receive the promise of the [Holy] Spirit.

Gal. 3:29 And if you belong to Christ, then you are Abraham's offspring and heirs according to promise.

Blood of Christ

Ex. 12:13 The blood shall be for a token or sign to you upon [the doorposts of] the houses where you are, [that] when I see the blood, I will pass over you, and no plague shall be upon you to destroy you when I smite the land of Egypt. [1 Cor. 5:7; Heb. 11:28.]

Matt. 26:27 And He took a cup, and when He had given thanks, He gave it to them, saying, Drink of it, all of you;

1 Cor. 11:28 Let a man [thoroughly] examine himself, and [only when he has done] so should he eat of the bread and drink of the cup.

Eph. 1:7 In Him we have redemption through His blood, the remission of our offenses, in accordance with the riches and the generosity of His gracious favor,

Eph. 2:13 But now in Christ Jesus, you who once were [so] far away, through (by, in) the blood of Christ have been brought near.

Heb. 9:14 How much more surely shall the blood of Christ, Who by virtue of [His] eternal Spirit has offered Himself as an unblemished sacrifice to God, purify our consciences from dead works and lifeless observances to serve the living God?

Heb. 9:20 Saying these words: This is the blood that seals and ratifies the agreement which God commanded [me to deliver to] you. [Exod. 24:6-8.]

1 Peter 1:18 You must know that you were redeemed from the useless way of living inherited by tradition from forefathers, not with corruptible things such as silver and gold,

1 Peter 1:19 But [you were purchased] with the precious blood of Christ, like that of a lamb without blemish or spot.

1 John 1:7 But if we are living and walking in the Light, as He is in the Light, we have fellowship with one another, and the blood of Jesus Christ His Son cleanses [removes] us from all sin and guilt.

Children

Ps. 127:3 Behold, children are a heritage from the Lord, the fruit of the womb a reward.

Ps. 127:5 Happy, blessed, and fortunate is the man whose quiver is filled with them! They will not be put to shame when they speak with their adversaries [in gatherings] at the [city's] gate.

Ps. 139:13 For You did form my inward parts; You did knit me together in my mother's womb.

Ps. 139:14 I will confess and praise You for You are fearful and wonderful and for the awful wonder of my birth! Wonderful are Your works, and that my inner self knows right well. My frame was not hidden from You when I was made in secret and skillfully wrought in the lowest parts of the earth.

Deut. 28:1 IF YOU will listen diligently to the voice of the Lord your God, being watchful to do all His commandments which I command you this day, the Lord your God will set you high above all the nations of the earth.

Deut. 28:2 And all these blessings shall come upon you and overtake you if you heed the voice of the Lord your God.

Deut. 28:3 Blessed shall you be in the city and blessed shall you be in the field.

Deut. 28:4 Blessed shall be the fruit of your body and the fruit of your ground and the fruit of your beasts, the increase of your cattle and the young of your flock.

Ps. 139:7 Where could I go from Your Spirit? Or where could I flee from Your presence?

Ps. 139:8 If I ascend into heaven, You are there; If I make my bed in hell, behold, You are there

Ps. 139:9 If I take the wings of the morning or dwell in the uttermost parts of the sea,

Ps. 139:10 Even there shall Your hand lead me, and Your right hand shall hold me.

Deut. 7:12 And if you hearken to these precepts and keep and do them, the Lord your God will keep with you the covenant and the steadfast love which He swore to your fathers.

Deut. 7:13 And He will love you, bless you, and multiply you; He will also bless the fruit of your body and the fruit of your land, your grain, your new wine, and your oil, the increase of your cattle and the young of your flock in the land which He swore to your fathers to give you.

Deut. 7:14 You shall be blessed above all peoples; there shall not be male or female barren among you, or among your cattle.

Deut. 7:15 And the Lord will take away from you all sickness, and none of the evil diseases of Egypt which you knew will He put upon you, but will lay them upon all who hate you.

Job 1:10 Have You not put a hedge about him and his house and all that he has, on every side? You have conferred prosperity and happiness upon him in the work of his hands, and his possessions have increased in the land.

Matt. 18:18 Truly I tell you, whatever you forbid and declare to be improper and unlawful on earth must be what is already forbidden in heaven, and whatever you permit and declare proper and lawful on earth must be what is already permitted in heaven.

Ps. 12:7 You will keep them and preserve them, O Lord; You will guard and keep us from this [evil] generation forever.

Num. 6:24 The Lord bless you and watch, guard, and keep you;

Num. 6:26 The Lord lift up His countenance upon you and give you peace.

Eph. 3:16 that He would grant you, according to the riches of His glory, to be strengthened with might through His spirit in the inner man.

Eph. 3:17 that Christ may dwell in your hearts through faith that you being rooted and grounded in love

Eph. 3:18 may be able to comprehend with all the saints what is the length and width and depth and height

Eph. 3:19 to know the love of Christ, which passes knowledge, that you may be filled with all the fullness of God

Discernment

John 6:13 Therefore they gathered them up and filled twelve baskets with the fragments of the barley loaves which were left over by those who had eaten.

Heb. 4:12 For the word of God is living and powerful, and sharper than any two edged sword, piercing even to the division of soul and spirit, and of joints and marrow and is a discerner of the thoughts and intents of the heart

Ps. 119:130 The entrance and unfolding of Your words give light; their unfolding gives understanding to the simple.

Matt. 21:22 And whatever you ask for in prayer, having faith, believing, you will receive.

Col. 1:9 For this reason we also, since the day we heard it, do not cease to pray for you and ask that you may be filled with the knowledge of His will in all wisdom and spiritual understanding.

Eph. 5:11 Take no part in and have no fellowship with the fruitless deeds and enterprises of darkness, but instead expose and reprove and convict them.

1 Tim. 2:3 For such [praying] is good and right, and [it is] pleasing and acceptable to God our Savior,

1 Tim. 2:4 Who wishes all men to be saved and [increasingly] to perceive and recognize and discern and know precisely and correctly the [divine] Truth.

Prov. 1:1 THE PROVERBS [truths obscurely expressed, maxims, and parables] of Solomon son of David, king of Israel:

Prov. 1:2 That people may know skillful and godly Wisdom and instruction, discern and comprehend the words of understanding and insight,

Prov. 1:7 The reverent and worshipful fear of the Lord is the beginning and the principal and choice part of knowledge [its starting point and its essence]; but fools despise skillful and godly Wisdom, instruction, and discipline.

Prov. 10:14 Wise men store up knowledge [in mind and heart], but the mouth of the foolish is a present destruction.

Prov. 3:21 My son, let them not escape from your sight, but keep sound and godly Wisdom and discretion,

Prov. 3:22 And they will be life to your inner self, and a gracious ornament to your neck (your outer self).

Prov. 3:23 Then you will walk in your way securely and in confident trust, and you shall not dash your foot or stumble.

Prov. 3:24 When you lie down, you shall not be afraid; yes, you shall lie down, and your sleep shall be sweet.

Ps. 139:2 You know my downsitting and my uprising; You understand my thoughts afar off.

Ps. 139:23 Search me [thoroughly], O God, and know my heart! Try me and know my thoughts!

Ps. 139:24 And see if there is any wicked or hurtful way in me, and lead me in the way everlasting.

Dan. 2:22 He reveals the deep and secret things; He knows what is in the darkness, and the light dwells with Him!

Ps. 32:5 I acknowledged my sin to You, and my iniquity I did not hide. I said, I will confess my transgressions to the Lord -then You forgave me the guilt and iniquity of my sin. Selah!

1 John 1:9 If we admit that we have sinned and confess our sins, He is faithful and just and will forgive our sins [dismiss our lawlessness] and cleanse us from all unrighteousness.

Rom. 5:5 Such hope never disappoints or deludes or shames us, for God's love has been poured out in our hearts through the Holy Spirit Who has been given to us.

Phil. 1:9 And this I pray: that your love may abound yet more and more and extend to its fullest development in knowledge and all keen insight,

Phil. 1:10 So that you may surely learn to sense what is vital, and approve and prize what is excellent and of real value, and that you may be untainted and pure and unerring and blameless until the day of Christ [not stumbling nor causing others to stumble].

Emotional Health

Ps. 34:17 When the righteous cry for help, the Lord hears, and delivers them out of all their distress and troubles.

Ps. 34:18 The Lord is close to those who are of a broken heart and saves such as are crushed with sorrow for sin and are humbly and thoroughly penitent.

Ps. 147:3 He heals the brokenhearted and binds up their wounds.

Ps. 145:18 The Lord is near to all who call upon Him, to all who call upon Him sincerely and in truth.

Ps. 44:21 Would not God discover this? For He knows the secrets of the heart.

Ps. 111:4 He has made His wonderful works to be remembered; the Lord is gracious, merciful, and full of loving compassion.

Ps. 147:5 Great is our Lord and of great power; His understanding is inexhaustible and boundless.

2 Thess. 3:16 Now may the Lord of peace Himself grant you His peace [the peace of His kingdom] at all times and in all ways [under all circumstances and conditions, whatever comes]. The Lord [be] with you all.

Is. 40:11 He will feed His flock like a shepherd: He will gather the lambs in His arms, He will carry them in His bosom and will gently lead those that have their young.

Josh. 1:5 No man shall be able to stand before you all the days of your life. As I was with Moses, so I will be with you; I will not fail you or forsake you.

Rom. 8:38 For I am persuaded beyond doubt (am sure) that neither death nor life, nor angels nor principalities, nor things impending and threatening nor things to come, nor powers,

Rom. 8:39 Nor height nor depth, nor anything else in all creation will be able to separate us from the love of God which is in Christ Jesus our Lord.

Is. 38:15 But what can I say? For He has both spoken to me and He Himself has done it. I must go softly [as in solemn procession] all my years and my sleep has fled because of the bitterness of my soul.

Is. 38:16 O Lord, by these things men live; and in all these is the life of my spirit. O give me back my health and make me live!

1 John 1:9 If we confess our sins, He is faithful and just to forgive us our sins and to cleanse us from all unrighteousness.

Rom. 16:20 And the God of peace will soon crush Satan under your feet. The grace of our Lord Jesus Christ (the Messiah) be with you.

Ezek. 11:19 And I will give them one heart and I will put a new spirit within them; and I will take the stony heart out of their flesh, and will give them a heart of flesh

Prov. 14:30 A calm and undisturbed mind and heart are the life and health of the body, but envy, jealousy, and wrath are like rottenness of the bones.

Phil. 4:6 Do not fret or have any anxiety about anything, but in every circumstance and in everything, by prayer and petition, with thanksgiving, continue to make your wants known to God.

Ps. 139:23 Search me [thoroughly], O God, and know my heart! Try me and know my thoughts!

Ps. 139:24 And see if there is any wicked or hurtful way in me, and lead me in the way everlasting.

John 14:27 Peace I leave with you. My peace I give unto you, not as the world gives do I give to you. Let not your heart be troubled, neither let it be afraid.

Rom. 8:37 Yet amid all these things we are more than conquerors and gain a surpassing victory through Him Who loved us.

2 Tim. 1:7 For God did not give us a spirit of timidity, but of power and of love and of calm and well-balanced mind and discipline and self-control.

Gal. 5:16 But I say, walk and live in the [Holy] Spirit [responsive to and controlled and guided by the Spirit]; then you will certainly not gratify the cravings and desires of the flesh.

Rom. 8:6 Now the mind of the flesh is death. But the mind of the [Holy] Spirit is life and peace.

Prov. 23:7 For as he thinks in his heart, so is he. As one who reckons, he says to you, eat and drink, yet his heart is not with you.

2 Cor. 10:5 [Inasmuch as we] refute arguments and
theories and reasonings and every proud and lofty
thing that sets itself up against the [true] knowledge
of God; and we lead every thought and purpose
away captive into the obedience of Christ,

Is. 41:10 Fear not, for I am with you; do not look around
you in terror and be dismayed, for I am your God. I
will strengthen and harden you to difficulties, yes, I
will help you; yes, I will hold you up and retain you
with My [victorious] right hand of rightness and
justice.

Rom. 5:8 But God shows and clearly proves His [own]
love for us by the fact that while we were still sinners, Christ (the Messiah, the Anointed One) died
for us.

Rom. 2:11 For God shows no partiality

Ps. 27:10 Although my father and my mother have forsaken me, yet the Lord will take me up.

Eph. 4:31 Let all bitterness and indignation and wrath
and resentment and quarreling and slander be ban-
ished from you, with all malice.

Eph. 4:32 And become useful and helpful and kind to
one another, tenderhearted, forgiving one another, as
God in Christ forgave you.

Matt. 17:20 He said to them, Because of the littleness
of your faith. For truly I say to you, if you have faith
[that is living] like a grain of mustard seed, you can
say to this mountain, Move from here to yonder
place, and it will move; and nothing will be impossible to you.

Ps. 33:20 Our inner selves wait [earnestly] for the Lord;
He is our Help and our Shield.

Ps. 33:21 For in Him does our heart rejoice, because we
have trusted in His holy name.

Ps. 33:22 Let Your mercy and loving-kindness, O Lord, be upon us, in proportion to our waiting and hoping for You.

Heb. 4:13 And not a creature exists that is concealed from His sight, but all things are open and exposed, naked and defenseless to the eyes of Him with Whom we have to give account.

Heb. 4:14 Inasmuch then as we have a great High Priest Who has [already] ascended and passed through the heavens, Jesus the Son of God, let us hold fast our confession [of faith in Him].

Heb. 4:15 For we do not have a High Priest Who is unable to understand and sympathize and have a shared feeling with our weaknesses and infirmities and liability to the assaults of temptation, but One Who has been tempted in every respect as we are, yet without sinning.

Heb. 4:16 Let us then fearlessly and confidently and boldly draw near to the throne of grace, that we may receive mercy and find grace to help in good time for every need.

Ps. 30:2 O Lord my God, I cried to You and You have healed me.

1 Peter 5:7 Casting the whole of your care on Him, for He cares for you affectionately and cares about you watchfully. [Ps. 55:22.]

Phil. 4:6 Do not fret or have any anxiety about anything, but in every circumstance and in everything, by prayer and petition (definite requests), with thanksgiving, continue to make your wants known to God.

Phil. 4:7 And God's peace which transcends all understanding shall garrison and mount guard over your hearts and minds in Christ Jesus.

1 Cor. 2:16 For who has known or understood the mind of the Lord so as to guide and instruct Him and give Him knowledge? But we have the mind of Christ and do hold the thoughts of His heart. [Isa. 40:13.]

Col. 3:2 And set your minds and keep them set on what is above (the higher things), not on the things that are on the earth.

Is. 26:3 You will guard him and keep him in perfect and constant peace whose mind is stayed on You, because he commits himself to You, leans on You, and hopes confidently in You.

1 Peter 3:12 For the eyes of the Lord are upon the righteous, and His ears are attentive to their prayer. But the face of the Lord is against those who practice evil. [Ps. 34:12-16.]

2 Chr. 16:9 For the eyes of the Lord run to and fro throughout the whole earth to show Himself strong in behalf of those whose hearts are blameless toward Him. You have done foolishly in this; therefore, from now on you shall have wars.

Ps. 56:11 In God have I put my trust and confident reliance; I will not be afraid. What can man do to me?

Ps. 46:1 To the Chief Musician. [A Psalm] of the sons of Korah, set to treble voices. A song. GOD IS our Refuge and Strength [mighty and impenetrable to temptation], a very present and well-proved help in trouble.

Num. 6:26 The Lord lift up His [approving] countenance upon you and give you peace.

Faithfulness

Deut. 7:9 Know, recognize, and understand therefore that the Lord your God, He is God, the faithful God, Who keeps covenant and steadfast love and mercy with those who love Him and keep His commandments, to a thousand generations,

Mal. 3:6 For I am the Lord, I do not change; that is why you, O sons of Jacob, are not consumed.

Heb. 13:8 Jesus Christ is the same, yesterday, today, and forever.

Rom. 3:3 What if some did not believe and were without faith? Does their lack of faith and their faithlessness nullify and make ineffective and void the faithfulness of God and His fidelity [to His Word]?

Rom. 3:4 By no means! Let God be found true though every human being is false and a liar, as it is written, That You may be justified and shown to be upright in what You say, and prevail when You are judged [by sinful men].

2 Tim. 2:13 If we are faithless, He remains true, for He cannot deny Himself.

Deut. 32:4 He is the Rock, His work is perfect, for all His ways are law and justice. A God of faithfulness without breach or deviation, just and right is He.

Ps. 146:5 Happy is he who has the God of Jacob for his help, whose hope is in the Lord his God, [Gen. 32:30.]

Ps. 146:6 Who made heaven and earth, the sea, and all that is in them, Who keeps truth and is faithful forever,

Ps. 92:2 To show forth Your loving-kindness in the morning and Your faithfulness by night,

2 Peter 1:3 For His divine power has bestowed upon us all things that to life and godliness, through the knowledge of Him Who called us by and to His own glory and excellence (virtue).

2 Peter 1:4 By means of these He has bestowed on us His precious and exceedingly great promises, so that through them you may escape from the moral decay that is in the world because of covetousness, and become sharers of the divine nature.

Is. 55:11 So shall My word be that goes forth out of My mouth: it shall not return to Me void, but it shall accomplish that which I please and purpose, and it shall prosper in the thing for which I sent it.

Ps. 119:114 You are my hiding place and my shield; I hope in Your word.

Heb. 10:23 So let us seize and hold fast and retain without wavering the hope we cherish and confess and our acknowledgement of it, for He Who promised is reliable (sure) and faithful to His word.

Favor of God

1 Cor. 1:30 But it is from Him that you have your life in Christ Jesus, Whom God made our Wisdom from God, our Righteousness, and our Consecration, and our Redemption [providing our ransom from eternal penalty for sin].

Acts 3:25 You are the descendants (sons) of the prophets and the heirs of the covenant which God made and gave to your forefathers, saying to Abraham, And in your Seed (Heir) shall all the families of the earth be blessed and benefited. [Gen. 22:18; Gal. 3:16.]

Ps. 5:12 For You, Lord, will bless the righteous; as with a shield You will surround him with goodwill.

Ps. 97:11 Light is sown for the righteous and strewn along their pathway, and joy for the upright in heart.

1 Tim. 1:14 And the grace of our Lord flowed out super-abundantly and beyond measure for me, accompanied by faith and love that are in Christ Jesus.

Col. 2:15 [God] disarmed the principalities and powers that were ranged against us and made a bold display and public example of them, in triumphing over them in Him and in it [the cross].

John 10:10 The thief comes only in order to steal and kill and destroy. I came that they may have and enjoy life, and have it in abundance.

Deut. 28:1 IF YOU will listen diligently to the voice of the Lord your God, being watchful to do all His commandments which I command you this day, the Lord your God will set you high above all the nations of the earth.

Deut. 28:2 And all these blessings shall come upon you and overtake you if you heed the voice of the Lord your God.

Deut. 28:3 Blessed shall you be in the city and blessed shall you be in the field.

Deut. 28:4 Blessed shall be the fruit of your body and the fruit of your ground and the fruit of your beasts, the increase of your cattle and the young of your flock.

Deut. 28:5 Blessed shall be your basket and your kneading trough.

Deut. 28:6 Blessed shall you be when you come in and blessed shall you be when you go out.

Deut. 28:7 The Lord shall cause your enemies who rise up against you to be defeated before your face; they shall come out against you one way and flee before you seven ways.

Deut. 28:8 The Lord shall command the blessing upon you in your storehouse and in all that you undertake. And He will bless you in the land which the Lord your God gives you.

Deut. 28:9 The Lord will establish you as a people holy to Himself, as He has sworn to you, if you keep the commandments of the Lord your God and walk in His ways.

Deut. 28:10 And all people of the earth shall see that you are called by the name [and in the presence of] the Lord, and they shall be afraid of you.

Deut. 28:11 And the Lord shall make you have a surplus of prosperity, through the fruit of your body, of your livestock, and of your ground, in the land which the Lord swore to your fathers to give you.

Deut. 28:12 The Lord shall open to you His good treasury, the heavens, to give the rain of your land in its season and to bless all the work of your hands; and you shall lend to many nations, but you shall not borrow.

Deut. 28:13 And the Lord shall make you the head, and not the tail; and you shall be above only, and you shall not be beneath, if you heed the commandments of the Lord your God which I command you this day and are watchful to do them.

Ps. 112:1 PRAISE THE Lord! Blessed is the man who fears [reveres and worships] the Lord, who delights greatly in His commandments. [Deut. 10:12.]

Ps. 112:2 His [spiritual] offspring shall be mighty upon earth; the generation of the upright shall be blessed.

Ps. 112:3 Prosperity and welfare are in his house, and his righteousness endures forever.

Ps. 112:4 Light arises in the darkness for the upright, gracious, compassionate, and just.

Ps. 84:11 For the Lord God is a Sun and Shield;
the Lord bestows grace and favor and glory! No
good thing will He withhold from those who walk
uprightly.

Ps. 84:12 O Lord of hosts, blessed is the man who
trusts in You!

Finances

Jer. 17:7 [Most] blessed is the man who believes in,
trusts in, and relies on the Lord, and whose hope and
confidence the Lord is.

Ps. 37:4 Delight yourself also in the Lord, and He will
give you the desires and secret petitions of your
heart.

Ps. 84:11 For the Lord God is a Sun and Shield; the
Lord bestows grace and favor and glory (honor,
splendor, and heavenly bliss)! No good thing will
He withhold from those who walk uprightly.

Matt. 6:8 Do not be like them, for your Father knows
what you need before you ask Him.

Phil. 4:19 And my God will liberally supply your every
need according to His riches in glory in Christ
Jesus.

3 John 1:2 Beloved, I pray that you may prosper in every
way and [that your body] may keep well, even as [I
know] your soul keeps well and prospers.

Mal. 3:10 Bring all the tithes (the whole tenth of your
income) into the storehouse, that there may be
food in My house, and prove Me now by it, says
the Lord of hosts, if I will not open the windows
of heaven for you and pour you out a blessing, that
there shall not be room enough to receive it.

2 Cor. 9:6 [Remember] this: he who sows sparingly and grudgingly will also reap sparingly and grudgingly, and he who sows generously will also reap generously and with blessings.

2 Cor. 9:7 Let each one as he has made up his own mind and purposed in his heart, not reluctantly or sorrowfully or under compulsion, for God loves a cheerful giver.

James 1:17 Every good gift and every perfect gift is from above; it comes down from the Father of all light, in [the shining of] Whom there can be no variation or shadow cast by His turning [as in an eclipse].

Heb. 13:5 Let your conduct be without covetousness, be content with such things as you have. For He Himself has said, "I will never leave you nor forsake you."

1 Tim. 6:10 For the love of money is a root of all evils; it is through this craving that some have been led astray and have wandered from the faith and pierced themselves through with many acute [mental] pangs.

Matt. 6:19 Do not gather and heap up and store up for yourselves treasures on earth, where moth and rust and worm consume and destroy, and where thieves break through and steal.

Matt. 6:20 But gather and heap up and store for yourselves treasures in heaven, where neither moth nor rust nor worm consume and destroy, and where thieves do not break through and steal;

Matt. 6:21 For where your treasure is, there will your heart be also.

1 Tim. 6:18 Let them do good, that they be rich in this present age not to be haughty, nor to trust in uncertain riches, but in the living God, who gives us richly all things to enjoy,

1 Tim. 6:19 storing up for themselves a good foundation for the time to come, that they may lay hold on
eternal life

2 Cor. 9:10 And [God] Who provides seed for the
sower and bread for eating will also provide and
multiply your sowing and increase the fruits of your
righteousness.

Forgiveness for Others

Matt. 6:14 For if you forgive people their trespasses,
your heavenly Father will also forgive you.

Matt. 6:15 But if you do not forgive others their trespasses, neither will your Father forgive you your
trespasses.

Rom. 1:5 It is through Him that we have received grace
(God's unmerited favor) and [our] apostleship to
promote obedience to the faith and make disciples
for His name's sake among all the nations,

Luke 17:3 Take heed to yourselves, if your brother sins
against you, rebuke him and if he repents, forgive
him

Luke 17:4 "And if he sins against you seven times in a
day and seven times in a day returns to you saying
"I repent," you shall forgive him.

1 Peter 4:8 Above all things have intense and unfailing
love for one another, for love covers a multitude of
sins .

Prov. 22:23 For the Lord will plead their cause and
deprive of life those who deprive [the poor or
afflicted].

Rom. 12:19 Beloved, never avenge yourselves, but leave
the way open for [God's] wrath; for it is written,
Vengeance is Mine, I will repay (requite), says the
Lord.

Acts 13:47 For so the Lord has charged us, saying, I have set you to be a light for the Gentiles, that you may bring salvation to the uttermost parts of the earth.

1 Cor. 13:5 It is not conceited; it is not rude and does not act unbecomingly. Love does not insist on its own rights or its own way, for it is not self-seeking; it is not touchy or fretful or resentful; it takes no account of the evil done to it.

Lev. 19:18 You shall not take revenge or bear any grudge against the sons of your people, but you shall love your neighbor as yourself. I am the Lord.

James 1:19 Understand, my beloved brethren. Let every man be quick to hear, slow to speak, slow to take offense and to get angry.

James 1:20 For man's anger does not promote the righteousness God [wishes and requires].

1 Cor. 13:7 Love bears up under anything and everything that comes, is ever ready to believe the best of every person, its hopes are fadeless under all circumstances, and it endures everything [without weakening].

Gal. 5:22 But the fruit of the [Holy] Spirit is love, joy, peace, patience, kindness, goodness, faithfulness,

Gal. 5:23 Gentleness, self-control. Against such things there is no law.

Heb. 12:15 Exercise foresight and be on the watch to look, to see that no one falls back from and fails to secure God's grace, in order that no root of resentment shoots forth and causes trouble and bitter torment, and the many become contaminated and defiled by it—

Lev. 19:16 You shall not go up and down as a dispenser of gossip and scandal among your people, nor shall you endanger the life of your neighbor. I am the Lord.

Lev. 19:17 You shall not hate your brother in your heart; but you shall surely rebuke your neighbor, lest you incur sin because of him.

Col. 3:8 But now put away and rid yourselves [completely] of all these things: anger, rage, bad feeling toward others, curses and slander, and foulmouthed abuse and shameful utterances from your lips!

Phil. 4:8 For the rest, brethren, whatever is true, whatever is worthy of reverence and is honorable and seemly, whatever is just, whatever is pure, whatever is lovely and lovable, whatever is kind and winsome and gracious, if there is any virtue and excellence, if there is anything worthy of praise, think on and weigh and take account of these things [fix your minds on them].

Matt. 5:44 But I tell you, Love your enemies and pray for those who persecute you,

Luke 6:28 Invoke blessings upon and pray for the happiness of those who curse you, implore God's blessing upon those who abuse you.

Forgiveness for Self

Ps. 32:1 [A Psalm of David.] A skillful song, or a didactic or reflective poem. BLESSED is he who has forgiveness of his transgression continually exercised upon him, whose sin is covered.

Rom. 8:1 THEREFORE, there is now no condemnation for those who are in Christ Jesus, who live and walk not after the dictates of the flesh, but after the dictates of the Spirit.

Ps. 32:5 I acknowledged my sin to You, and my iniquity I did not hide. I said, I will confess my transgressions to the Lord -then You forgave me the guilt and iniquity of my sin. Selah [pause, and calmly think of that]!

Phil. 3:13 I do not consider, brethren, that I have captured and made it my own [yet]; but one thing I do: forgetting what lies behind and straining forward to what lies ahead,

2 Cor. 5:17 Therefore if any person is in Christ he is a new creation; the old has passed away. Behold, the fresh and new has come!

Is. 61:10 I will greatly rejoice in the Lord, my soul will exult in my God; for He has clothed me with the garments of salvation, He has covered me with the robe of righteousness, as a bridegroom decks himself with a garland, and as a bride adorns herself with her jewels.

Col. 3:12 Clothe yourselves therefore, as God's own chosen ones– purified, holy and well-beloved–with tenderhearted pity and mercy, kind feeling, a lowly opinion of yourselves, gentle ways, [and] patience.

2 Cor. 5:21 For our sake He made Christ to be sin Who knew no sin, so that in and through Him we might become the righteousness of God.

2 Cor. 12:9 But He said to me, My grace is enough for you; for My strength and power are made perfect and show themselves most effective in [your] weakness. Therefore, I will all the more gladly glory in my weaknesses and infirmities, that the strength and power of Christ may rest upon me!

Rom. 8:37 Yet amid all these things we are more than conquerors and gain a surpassing victory through Him Who loved us.

2 Cor. 10:5 [Inasmuch as we] refute arguments and theories and reasonings and every proud and lofty thing that sets itself up against the [true] knowledge of God; and we lead every thought and purpose away captive into the obedience of Christ (the Messiah, the Anointed One),

Ps. 103:14 For He knows our frame, He [earnestly] remembers and imprints [on His heart] that we are dust.

2Jo 1:6 And what this love consists in is this: that we live and walk in accordance with and guided by His commandments. This is the commandment, as you have heard from the beginning, that you continue to walk in love.

Ps. 139:13 For You did form my inward parts; You did knit me together in my mother's womb.

Jer. 29:11 For I know the thoughts and plans that I have for you, says the Lord, thoughts and plans for welfare and peace and not for evil, to give you hope in your final outcome.

Ps. 139:16 Your eyes saw my unformed substance, and in Your book all the days [of my life] were written before ever they took shape, when as yet there was none of them.

Forgiveness of God

Ps. 86:5 For You, O Lord, are good, and ready to forgive [our trespasses, sending them away, letting them go completely and forever]; and You are abundant in mercy and loving-kindness to all those who call upon You.

Rom. 10:12 [No one] for there is no distinction between Jew and Greek. The same Lord is Lord over all and He generously bestows His riches upon all who call upon Him.

Rom. 10:13 For everyone who calls upon the name of the Lord [invoking Him as Lord] will be saved.

John 3:17 For God did not send the Son into the world in order to judge the world, but that the world might find salvation and be made safe and sound through Him.

Rom. 10:9 Because if you acknowledge and confess with your lips that Jesus is Lord and in your heart believe that God raised Him from the dead, you will be saved.

Ps. 103:10 He has not dealt with us after our sins nor rewarded us according to our iniquities.

Ps. 103:11 For as the heavens are high above the earth, so great are His mercy and loving-kindness toward those who reverently and worshipfully fear Him.

Ps. 103:12 As far as the east is from the west, so far has He removed our transgressions from us.

Is. 43:25 I, even I, am He Who blots out and cancels your transgressions, for My own sake, and I will not remember your sins.

1 John 1:5 And this is the message which we have heard from Him and now are reporting to you: God is Light, and there is no darkness in Him at all.

1 John 1:7 But if we [really] are living and walking in the Light, as He [Himself] is in the Light, we have [true, unbroken] fellowship with one another, and the blood of Jesus Christ His Son cleanses us from all sin and guilt.

Titus 3:4 But when the goodness and loving-kindness of God our Savior to man [as man] appeared,

Titus 3:5 He saved us, not because of any works of righteousness that we had done, but because of His own pity and mercy, by [the] cleansing [bath] of the new birth (regeneration) and renewing of the Holy Spirit,

Titus 3:6 Which He poured out [so] richly upon us through Jesus Christ our Savior.

Titus 3:7 [And He did it in order] that we might be justified by His grace, [that we might be acknowledged and counted as conformed to the divine will in purpose, thought, and action], and that we might become heirs of eternal life according to [our] hope.

Generational Curses

Rom. 5:8 But God shows and clearly proves His [own] love for us by the fact that while we were still sinners, Christ (the Messiah, the Anointed One) died for us.

Rom. 5:10 For if while we were enemies we were reconciled to God through the death of His Son, it is much more [certain], now that we are reconciled, that we shall be saved (daily delivered from sin's dominion) through His [resurrection] life.

John 1:13 Who owe their birth neither to bloods nor to the will of the flesh nor to the will of man [that of a natural father], but to God.

1 Peter 1:4 [Born anew] into an inheritance which is beyond the reach of change and decay

Ex. 20:3 You shall have no other gods before or besides Me.

Ex. 20:4 You shall not make yourself any graven image [to worship it] or any likeness of anything that is in the heavens above, or that is in the earth beneath, or that is in the water under the earth;

Ex. 20:5 You shall not bow down yourself to them or serve them; for I the Lord your God am a jealous God, visiting the iniquity of the fathers upon the children to the third and fourth generation of those who hate Me, [Isa. 42:8; 48:11.]

2 Cor. 5:17 Therefore if any person is [ingrafted] in Christ (the Messiah) he is a new creation; the old [previous moral and spiritual condition] has passed away. Behold, the fresh and new has come!

Col. 2:14 Having cancelled and blotted out and wiped away the handwriting of the note with its legal decrees and demands which was in force and stood against us. This [note with its regulations, decrees, and demands] He set aside and cleared completely out of our way by nailing it to [His] cross.

Col. 2:15 [God] disarmed the principalities and powers that were ranged against us and made a bold display and public example of them, in triumphing over them in Him and in it [the cross].

2 Cor. 1:22 [He has also appropriated and acknowledged us as His by] putting His seal upon us and giving us His [Holy] Spirit in our hearts as the security deposit and guarantee [of the fulfillment of His promise].

Ex. 20:6 But showing mercy and steadfast love to a thousand generations of those who love Me and keep My commandments.

Ex. 34:6 And the Lord passed by before him, and proclaimed, The Lord! the Lord! a God merciful and gracious, slow to anger, and abundant in loving-kindness and truth,

Ex. 34:7 Keeping mercy and loving-kindness for thousands, forgiving iniquity and transgression and sin, but Who will by no means clear the guilty, visiting the iniquity of the fathers upon the children and the

children's children, to the third and fourth generation.

Ps. 119:90 Your faithfulness is from generation to
generation; You have established the earth, and it
stands fast.

Gratitude

Ps. 103:1 [A Psalm] of David. BLESS
[AFFECTIONATELY, gratefully praise] the
Lord, O my soul; and all that is [deepest] within me,
bless His holy name!

Ps. 69:30 I will praise the name of God with a song
and will magnify Him with thanksgiving,

Ps. 69:31 And it will please the Lord better than an ox
or a bullock that has horns and hoofs.

Ps. 100:4 Enter into His gates with thanksgiving and
a thank offering and into His courts with praise! Be
thankful and say so to Him, bless and affectionately
praise His name!

Is. 61:10 I will greatly rejoice in the Lord, my soul will
exult in my God; for He has clothed me with the
garments of salvation, He has covered me with the
robe of righteousness, as a bridegroom decks himself
with a garland, and as a bride adorns herself with
her jewels.

Ps. 68:19 Blessed be the Lord, Who bears our burdens
and carries us day by day, even the God Who is our
salvation! Selah [pause, and calmly think of that]!

Heb. 7:25 Therefore He is able also to save to the
uttermost those who come to God through Him,
since He is always living to make petition to God
and intercede with Him and intervene for them.

John 8:12 Once more Jesus addressed the crowd. He said, I am the Light of the world. He who follows Me will not be walking in the dark, but will have the Light which is Life.

Heb. 13:5 Let your character or moral disposition be free from love of money [including greed, avarice, lust, and craving for earthly possessions] and be satisfied with your present [circumstances and with what you have]; for He [God] Himself has said, I will not in any way fail you nor give you up nor leave you without support. [I will] not, [I will] not, [I will] not in any degree leave you helpless nor forsake nor let [you] down (relax My hold on you)! [Assuredly not!]

Deut. 7:9 Know, recognize, and understand therefore that the Lord your God, He is God, the faithful God, Who keeps covenant and steadfast love and mercy with those who love Him and keep His commandments, to a thousand generations,

Mal. 3:6 For I am the Lord, I do not change; that is why you, O sons of Jacob, are not consumed.

Rom. 8:32 He who did not withhold or spare [even] His own Son but gave Him up for us all, will He not also with Him freely and graciously give us all [other] things?

Phil. 4:19 And my God will liberally supply (fill to the full) your every need according to His riches in glory in Christ Jesus.

Ps. 103:2 Bless (affectionately, gratefully praise) the Lord, O my soul, and forget not [one of] all His benefits—

Ps. 103:3 Who forgives [every one of] all your iniquities, Who heals [each one of] all your diseases,

Ps. 103:4 Who redeems your life from the pit and corruption, Who beautifies, dignifies, and crowns you
with loving-kindness and tender mercy;

Ps. 103:5 Who satisfies your mouth [your necessity
and desire at your personal age and situation] with
good so that your youth, renewed, is like the eagle's
[strong, overcoming, soaring]! [Isa. 40:31.]

Ps. 103:6 The Lord executes righteousness and justice
[not for me only, but] for all who are oppressed.

Ps. 103:7 He made known His ways [of righteousness
and justice] to Moses, His acts to the children of
Israel.

Ps. 103:8 The Lord is merciful and gracious, slow to
anger and plenteous in mercy and loving-kindness.

Ps. 103:9 He will not always chide or be contending,
neither will He keep His anger forever or hold a
grudge.

Ps. 103:10 He has not dealt with us after our sins nor
rewarded us according to our iniquities.

Ps. 98:1 A Psalm. O SING to the Lord a new song,
for He has done marvelous things; His right hand
and His holy arm have wrought salvation for Him.

Ps. 89:13 You have a mighty arm; strong is Your hand,
Your right hand is soaring high.

Ps. 63:8 My whole being follows hard after You and
clings closely to You; Your right hand upholds me.

Heb. 13:5 Let your character or moral disposition be
free from love of money [including greed, avarice,
lust, and craving for earthly possessions] and be
satisfied with your present [circumstances and with
what you have]; for He [God] Himself has said,
I will not in any way fail you nor give you up nor
leave you without support. I will not in any degree
leave you helpless nor forsake nor let [you] down!
[Assuredly not!]

Rom. 8:28 We are assured and know that [God being a partner in their labor] all things work together and are [fitting into a plan] for good to and for those who love God and are called according to [His] design and purpose.

Eph. 5:19 Speak out to one another in psalms and hymns and spiritual songs, offering praise with voices [and instruments] and making melody with all your heart to the Lord,

Eph. 5:20 At all times and for everything giving thanks in the name of our Lord Jesus Christ to God the Father.

Guidance

Jer. 29:11 For I know the thoughts and plans that I have for you, says the Lord, thoughts and plans for welfare and peace and not for evil, to give you hope in your final outcome.

Ps. 139:3 You sift and search out my path and my lying down, and You are acquainted with all my ways.

Ps. 23:3 He refreshes and restores my life (my self); He leads me in the paths of righteousness [uprightness and right standing with Him—not for my earning it, but] for His name's sake.

2 Tim. 1:9 [For it is He] Who delivered and saved us and called us with a calling in itself holy and leading to holiness; not because of anything of merit that we have done, but because of and to further His own purpose and grace which was given us in Christ Jesus before the world began.

Prov. 3:5 Lean on, trust in, and be confident in the Lord with all your heart and mind and do not rely on your own insight or understanding.

Prov. 3:6 In all your ways know, recognize, and acknowledge Him, and He will direct and make straight and plain your paths.

Ps. 1:1 BLESSED is the man who walks and lives not in the counsel of the ungodly, nor stands [submissive and inactive] in the path where sinners walk, nor sits down [to relax and rest] where the scornful [and the mockers] gather.

Ps. 1:2 But his delight and desire are in the law of the Lord, and on His law (the precepts, the instructions, the teachings of God) he habitually meditates (ponders and studies) by day and by night. [Rom. 13:8-10; Gal. 3:1-29; 2 Tim. 3:16.]

Ps. 1:3 And he shall be like a tree firmly planted [and tended] by the streams of water, ready to bring forth its fruit in its season; its leaf also shall not fade or wither; and everything he does shall prosper [and come to maturity].

John 16:13 But when He, the Spirit of Truth comes, He will guide you into all the Truth. For He will not speak His own message; but He will tell whatever He hears [from the Father; He will give the message that has been given to Him], and He will announce and declare to you the things that are to come [that will happen in the future].

John 14:26 But the Comforter (Counselor, Helper, Intercessor, Advocate, Strengthener, Standby), the Holy Spirit, Whom the Father will send in My name [in My place, to represent Me and act on My behalf], He will teach you all things. And He will cause you to recall everything I have told you.

Ps. 37:7 Be still and rest in the Lord; wait for Him and patiently lean yourself upon Him; fret not yourself because of him who prospers in his way, because of the man who brings wicked devices to pass.

Is. 55:9 For as the heavens are higher than the earth, so are My ways higher than your ways and My thoughts than your thoughts.

Ps. 18:30 As for God, His way is perfect! The word of the Lord is tested and tried; He is a shield to all those who take refuge and put their trust in Him.

Ps. 119:105 Your word is a lamp to my feet and a light to my path. [Prov. 6:23.]

Ps. 147:11 The Lord takes pleasure in those who reverently and worshipfully fear Him, in those who hope in His mercy and loving-kindness. [Ps. 145:20.]

Ps. 37:23 The steps of a [good] man are directed and established by the Lord when He delights in his way [and He busies Himself with his every step].

James 1:5 If any of you is deficient in wisdom, let him ask of the giving God [Who gives] to everyone liberally and ungrudgingly, without reproaching or faultfinding, and it will be given him.

Prov. 4:11 I have taught you in the way of skillful and godly Wisdom [which is comprehensive insight into the ways and purposes of God]; I have led you in paths of uprightness.

Prov. 4:12 When you walk, your steps shall not be hampered [your path will be clear and open]; and when you run, you shall not stumble.

Ps. 32:8 I [the Lord] will instruct you and teach you in the way you should go; I will counsel you with My eye upon you.

Ps. 31:3 Yes, You are my Rock and my Fortress; therefore for Your name's sake lead me and guide me.

Is. 58:11 And the Lord shall guide you continually and satisfy you in drought and in dry places and make strong your bones. And you shall be like a watered garden and like a spring of water whose waters fail not.

Prov. 3:26 For the Lord shall be your confidence, firm
and strong, and shall keep your foot from being
caught [in a trap or some hidden danger].

Ps. 139:5 You have beset me and shut me in—behind
and before, and You have laid Your hand upon me.

Deut. 31:8 It is the Lord Who goes before you; He will
[march] with you; He will not fail you or let you go
or forsake you; [let there be no cowardice or flinch-
ing, but] fear not, neither become broken [in spirit—
depressed, dismayed, and unnerved with alarm].

Jude 1:24 Now to Him Who is able to keep you without stumbling or slipping or falling, and to present
[you] unblemished (blameless and faultless) before
the presence of His glory in triumphant joy and
exultation [with unspeakable, ecstatic delight]—

Jude 1:25 To the only God, our Savior through Jesus
Christ our Lord, be glory (splendor), majesty, might
and dominion, and power and authority, before all
time and now and forever (unto all the ages of eter-
nity). Amen (so be it).

Healing

Is. 41:10 Fear not, for I am with you; do not look around
you in terror and be dismayed, for I am your God. I
will strengthen and harden you to difficulties, yes, I
will help you; yes, I will hold you up and retain you
with My [victorious] right hand of rightness and
justice.

Is. 53:5 But He was wounded for our transgressions,
He was bruised for our guilt and iniquities; the
chastisement peace and well-being for us was upon
Him, and with the stripes [that wounded] Him we
are healed and made whole.

Is. 54:17 But no weapon that is formed against you shall prosper, and every tongue that shall rise against you in judgment you shall show to be in the wrong. This [peace, righteousness, security, triumph over opposition] is the heritage of the servants of the Lord [those in whom the ideal Servant of the Lord is reproduced]; this is the righteousness or the vindication which they obtain from Me [this is that which I impart to them as their justification], says the Lord.

Is. 58:8 Then shall your light break forth like the morning, and your healing [your restoration and the power of a new life] shall spring forth speedily; your righteousness [your rightness, your justice, and your right relationship with God] shall go before you [conducting you to peace and prosperity], and the glory of the Lord shall be your rear guard.

Mal. 4:2 But unto you who revere and worshipfully fear My name shall the Sun of Righteousness arise with healing in His wings and His beams, and you shall go forth and leap like calves [released] from the stall.

Matt 4:23 And He went about all Galilee, teaching in their synagogues and preaching the good news [Gospel] of the kingdom, and healing every disease and every weakness and infirmity among the people.

Matt 15:13 He answered, Every plant which My heavenly Father has not planted will be torn up by the roots.

Ps. 145:1 I WILL extol You, my God, O King; and I will bless Your name forever and ever [with grateful, affectionate praise].

Acts 9:34 And Peter said to him, Aeneas, Jesus Christ (the Messiah) [now] makes you whole. Get up and make your bed! And immediately [Aeneas] stood up.

Acts 14:9 He was listening to Paul as he talked, and [Paul] gazing intently at him and observing that he had faith to be healed,

James 5:15 And the prayer [that is] of faith will save him who is sick, and the Lord will restore him; and if he has committed sins, he will be forgiven.

Ex. 12:7 They shall take of the blood and put it on the two side posts and on the lintel [above the door space] of the houses in which they shall eat [the Passover lamb].

Ex. 12:13 The blood shall be for a token or sign to you upon [the doorposts of] the houses where you are, [that] when I see the blood, I will pass over you, and no plague shall be upon you to destroy you when I smite the land of Egypt.

Ex. 15:26 Saying, If you will diligently hearken to the voice of the Lord your God and will do what is right in His sight, and will listen to and obey His commandments and keep all His statutes, I will put none of the diseases upon you which I brought upon the Egyptians, for I am the Lord Who heals you.

Gal. 3:13 Christ purchased our freedom [redeeming us] from the curse (doom) of the Law [and its condemnation] by [Himself] becoming a curse for us, for it is written [in the Scriptures], Cursed is everyone who hangs on a tree (is crucified);

Gal. 3:14 To the end that through [their receiving] Christ Jesus, the blessing [promised] to Abraham might come upon the Gentiles, so that we through faith might [all] receive [the realization of] the promise of the [Holy] Spirit.

1 Cor 6:19 Do you not know that your body is the temple of the Holy Spirit Who lives within you, Whom you have received [as a Gift] from God? You are not your own,

Luke 4:40 Now at the setting of the sun [indicating the end of the Sabbath], all those who had any [who were] sick with various diseases brought them to Him, and He laid His hands upon every one of them and cured them.

Healthy Pregnancy

Ps. 127:3 Behold, children are a heritage from the Lord, the fruit of the womb a reward.

Ps. 139:13 For You did form my inward parts; You did knit me together in my mother's womb.

Prov. 4:21 Let them not depart from your sight; keep them in the center of your heart.

Prov. 4:22 For they are life to those who find them, healing and health to all their flesh.

Job 1:10 Have You not put a hedge about him and his house and all that he has, on every side? You have conferred prosperity and happiness upon him in the work of his hands, and his possessions have increased in the land.

Is. 54:17 But no weapon that is formed against you shall prosper, and every tongue that shall rise against you in judgment you shall show to be in the wrong. This [peace, righteousness, security, triumph over opposition] is the heritage of the servants of the Lord [those in whom the ideal Servant of the Lord is reproduced]; this is the righteousness or the vindication which they obtain from Me [this is that which I impart to them as their justification], says the Lord.

Ps. 91:11 For He will give His angels [especial] charge over you to accompany and defend and preserve you in all your ways [of obedience and service].

Matt. 18:10 Beware that you do not despise or feel scornful toward or think little of one of these little ones, for I tell you that in heaven their angels always are in the presence of and look upon the face of My Father Who is in heaven.

Jer. 29:11 For I know the thoughts and plans that I have for you, says the Lord, thoughts and plans for welfare and peace and not for evil, to give you hope in your final outcome.

Deut. 5:29 Oh, that they had such a [mind and] heart in them always [reverently] to fear Me and keep all My commandments, that it might go well with them and with their children forever!

Deut. 12:25 You shall not eat it, that all may go well with you and with your children after you, when you do what is right in the sight of the Lord.

Gen. 1:27 So God created man in His own image, in the image and likeness of God He created him; male and female He created them.

Ps. 147:13 For He has strengthened and made hard the bars of your gates, and He has blessed your children within you.

Hope

I Cor 13:7 Love bears up under anything and everything that comes, is ever ready to believe the best of every person, its hopes are fadeless under all circumstances, and it endures everything [without weakening].

1 Cor 13:13 And so faith, hope, love abide [faith—conviction and belief respecting man's relation to God and divine things; hope—joyful and confident expectation of eternal salvation; love—true affection for God and man, growing out of God's love for and in us], these three; but the greatest of these is love.

Titus 2:13 Awaiting and looking for the [fulfillment, the realization of our] blessed hope, even the glorious appearing of our great God and Savior Christ Jesus [the Messiah, the Anointed One]

Rom. 5:2 Through Him also we have [our] access by faith into this grace [state of God's favor] in which we stand. And let us rejoice and exult in our hope of experiencing and enjoying the glory of God.

Rom. 5:4 And endurance (fortitude) develops maturity of character. And character [of this sort] produces [the habit of] joyful and confident hope of eternal salvation.

Rom. 8:25 But if we hope for what is still unseen by us, we wait for it with patience and composure.

Rom. 12:12 Rejoice and exult in hope; be steadfast and patient in suffering and tribulation; be constant in prayer.

Rom. 15:4 For whatever was thus written in former days was written for our instruction, that by [our steadfast and patient] endurance and the encourage-ment [drawn] from the Scriptures we might hold fast to and cherish hope.

Is. 25:9 It shall be said in that day, Behold our God upon Whom we have waited and hoped, that He might save us! This is the Lord, we have waited for Him; we will be glad and rejoice in His salvation.

Is. 26:3 You will guard him and keep him in perfect and constant peace whose mind [both its inclination and its character] is stayed on You, because he commits himself to You, leans on You, and hopes confidently in You.

Acts 17:27 So that they should seek God, in the hope that they might feel after Him and find Him, although He is not far from each one of us.

Ps. 22:9 Yet You are He Who took me out of the womb; You made me hope and trust when I was on my mother's breasts.

Ps. 25:2 O my God, I trust, lean on, rely on, and am confident in You. Let me not be put to shame or [my hope in You] be disappointed; let not my enemies triumph over me.

Ps. 27:14 Wait and hope for and expect the Lord; be brave and of good courage and let your heart be stout and enduring. Yes, wait for and hope for and expect the Lord.

Ps. 32:7 You are a hiding place for me; You, Lord, preserve me from trouble; You surround me with songs and shouts of deliverance. Selah

Ps. 33:18 Behold, the Lord's eye is upon those who fear Him [who revere and worship Him with awe], who wait for Him and hope in His mercy and loving-kindness,

Ps. 42:5 Why are you cast down, O my inner self? And why should you moan over me and be disquieted within me? Hope in God and wait expectantly for Him, for I shall yet praise Him, my Help and my God.

Ps. 52:9 I will thank You and confide in You forever, because You have done it [delivered me and kept me safe]. I will wait on, hope in and expect in Your name, for it is good, in the presence of Your saints.

Ps. 71:14 But I will hope continually, and will praise You yet more and more.

Gen. 50:21 Now therefore, do not be afraid. I will provide for and support you and your little ones. And he comforted them [imparting cheer, hope, strength] and spoke to their hearts [kindly].

Infertility

Eph. 3:20 Now to Him Who, by (in consequence of) the [action of His] power that is at work within us, is able to [carry out His purpose and] do superabundantly, far over and above all that we [dare] ask or think [infinitely beyond our highest prayers, desires, thoughts, hopes, or dreams]—

Heb. 4:12 For the Word that God speaks is alive and full of power [making it active, operative, energizing, and effective]; it is sharper than any two-edged sword, penetrating to the dividing line of the breath of life and spirit, and of joints and marrow, exposing and sifting and analyzing and judging the very thoughts and purposes of the heart.

Eph. 1:19 And [so that you can know and understand] what is the immeasurable and unlimited and unsurpassing greatness of His power in and for us who believe, as demonstrated in the working of His mighty strength,

Rom. 8:11 And if the Spirit of Him Who raised up Jesus from the dead dwells in you, [then] He Who raised up Christ Jesus from the dead will also restore to life your mortal bodies through His Spirit Who dwells in you.

Gen. 17:19 But God said, Sarah your wife shall bear you a son indeed, and you shall call his name Isaac [laughter]; and I will establish My covenant or solemn pledge with him for an everlasting covenant and with his posterity after him.

Gen. 21:1 THE LORD visited Sarah as He had said, and the Lord did for her as He had promised.

Ps. 37:4 Delight yourself also in the Lord, and He will give you the desires and secret petitions of your heart.

Ps. 145:16 You open Your hand and satisfy every living thing with favor.

Ps. 145:17 The Lord is [rigidly] righteous in all His ways and gracious and merciful in all His works.

Ps. 145:18 The Lord is near to all who call upon Him, to all who call upon Him sincerely and in truth.

Ps. 145:19 He will fulfill the desires of those who reverently and worshipfully fear Him; He also will hear their cry and will save them.

Rom. 4:17 As it is written, I have made you the father of many nations. [He was appointed our father] in the sight of God in Whom he believed, Who gives life to the dead and speaks of the nonexistent things that [He has foretold and promised] as if they [already] existed.

Rom. 4:18 [For Abraham, human reason for] hope being gone, hoped in faith that he should become the father of many nations, as he had been promised, So [numberless] shall your descendants be. [Gen. 15:5.]

Rom. 4:19 He did not weaken in faith when he considered the [utter] impotence of his own body, which was as good as dead because he was about a hundred years old, or [when he considered] the barrenness of Sarah's [deadened] womb.

Rom. 4:20 No unbelief or distrust made him waver concerning the promise of God, but he grew strong and was empowered by faith as he gave praise and glory to God,

Rom. 4:21 Fully satisfied and assured that God was able and mighty to keep His word and to do what He had promised.

Marriage

Matt 19:5 And said, For this reason a man shall leave his father and mother and shall be united firmly (joined inseparably) to his wife, and the two shall become one flesh?

Matt 19:6 So they are no longer two, but one flesh. What therefore God has joined together, let not man put asunder (separate).

Eph. 5:23 For the husband is head of the wife as Christ is the Head of the church, Himself the Savior of [His] body.

Eph. 5:24 As the church is subject to Christ, so let wives also be subject in everything to their husbands.

Eph. 5:25 Husbands, love your wives, as Christ loved the church and gave Himself up for her,

James 3:16 For wherever there is jealousy and contention, there will also be confusion and all sorts of evil and vile practices.

1 Pet. 3:7 In the same way you married men should live considerately with [your wives], with an intelligent recognition [of the marriage relation], honoring the woman as [physically] the weaker, but [realizing that you] are joint heirs of the grace [God's unmerited favor] of life, in order that your prayers may not be hindered and cut off. [Otherwise you cannot pray effectively.]

Rom. 5:5 Such hope never disappoints or deludes or shames us, for God's love has been poured out in our hearts through the Holy Spirit Who has been given to us.

1 Cor 13:4 Love endures long and is patient and kind; love never is envious nor boils over with jealousy, is not boastful or vainglorious, does not display itself haughtily.

1 Cor 13:5 It is not conceited (arrogant and inflated with pride); it is not rude (unmannerly) and does not act unbecomingly. Love (God's love in us) does not insist on its own rights or its own way, for it is not self-seeking; it is not touchy or fretful or resentful; it takes no account of the evil done to it [it pays no attention to a suffered wrong].

1 Cor 13:6 It does not rejoice at injustice and unrighteousness, but rejoices when right and truth prevail.

1 Cor 13:7 Love bears up under anything and everything that comes, is ever ready to believe the best of every person, its hopes are fadeless under all circumstances, and it endures everything [without weakening].

1 Cor 13:8 Love never fails [never fades out or becomes obsolete or comes to an end]. As for prophecy (the gift of interpreting the divine will and purpose), it will be fulfilled and pass away; as for tongues, they will be destroyed and cease; as for knowledge, it will pass away [it will lose its value and be superseded by truth].

Parenting

Mark 10:13 And they kept bringing young children to Him that He might touch them, and the disciples were reproving them [for it].

Mark 10:14 But when Jesus saw [it], He was indignant and pained and said to them, Allow the children to come to Me—do not forbid or prevent or hinder them—for to such belongs the kingdom of God.

Mark 10:15 Truly I tell you, whoever does not receive and accept and welcome the kingdom of God like a little child [does positively] shall not enter it at all.

Mark 10:16 And He took them [the children up one by one] in His arms and [fervently invoked a] blessing, placing His hands upon them.

Heb. 2:13 And again He says, My trust and assured reliance and confident hope shall be fixed in Him. And yet again, Here I am, I and the children whom God has given Me.

Prov. 22:6 Train up a child in the way he should go [and in keeping with his individual gift or bent], and when he is old he will not depart from it.

James 1:5 If any of you is deficient in wisdom, let him ask of the giving God [Who gives] to everyone liberally and ungrudgingly, without reproaching or faultfinding, and it will be given him.

Prov. 13:24 He who spares his rod hates his son, but he who loves him disciplines diligently and punishes him early.

Heb. 12:10 For [our earthly fathers] disciplined us for only a short period of time and chastised us as seemed proper and good to them; but He disciplines us for our certain good, that we may become sharers in His own holiness.

Prov. 19:18 Discipline your son while there is hope, but do not set yourself to his ruin.

Phil. 2:5 Let this same attitude and purpose and [humble] mind be in you which was in Christ Jesus: [Let Him be your example in humility:]

Heb. 12:11 For the time being no discipline brings joy, but seems grievous and painful; but afterwards it yields a peaceable fruit of righteousness to those who have been trained by it [a harvest of fruit which consists in righteousness—in conformity to God's will in purpose, thought, and action, resulting in right living and right standing with God].

Prov. 29:15 The rod and reproof give wisdom, but a
    child left undisciplined brings his mother to shame.

Prov. 29:17 Correct your son, and he will give you rest;
    yes, he will give delight to your heart.

1 Cor. 13:4 Love endures long and is patient and kind;
    love never is envious nor boils over with jealousy, is
    not boastful or vainglorious, does not display itself
    haughtily.

1 Cor. 13:5 It is not conceited; it is not rude and does
    not act unbecomingly. Love (God's love in us) does
    not insist on its own rights or its own way, for it is
    not self-seeking; it is not touchy or fretful or resent-
    ful; it takes no account of the evil done to it [it pays
    no attention to a suffered wrong].

1 Cor. 13:6 It does not rejoice at injustice and unrigh-
    teousness, but rejoices when right and truth prevail.

1 Cor. 13:7 Love bears up under anything and every-
    thing that comes, is ever ready to believe the best
    of every person, its hopes are fadeless under all
    circumstances, and it endures everything [without
    weakening].

Col. 3:12 Clothe yourselves therefore, as God's own
    chosen ones [His own picked representatives], [who
    are] purified and holy and well-beloved [by God
    Himself, by putting on behavior marked by] tender-
    hearted pity and mercy, kind feeling, a lowly opinion
    of yourselves, gentle ways, [and] patience [which
    is tireless and long-suffering, and has the power to
    endure whatever comes, with good temper].

Rom. 15:1 WE WHO are strong [in our convictions
    and of robust faith] ought to bear with the failings
    and the frailties and the tender scruples of the weak;
    [we ought to help carry the doubts and qualms of
    others] and not to please ourselves.

1 Thess. 5:14 And we earnestly beseech you, brethren, admonish (warn and seriously advise) those who are out of line [the loafers, the disorderly, and the unruly]; encourage the timid and fainthearted, help and give your support to the weak souls, [and] be very patient with everybody [always keeping your temper]. [Isa. 35:4.]

Lev. 19:18 You shall not take revenge or bear any grudge against the sons of your people, but you shall love your neighbor as yourself. I am the Lord.

Matt. 6:14 For if you forgive people their trespasses [their reckless and willful sins, leaving them, letting them go, and giving up resentment], your heavenly Father will also forgive you.

Col. 2:14 Having cancelled and blotted out and wiped away the handwriting of the note (bond) with its legal decrees and demands which was in force and stood against us (hostile to us). This [note with its regulations, decrees, and demands] He set aside and cleared completely out of our way by nailing it to [His] cross.

Deut. 6:7 You shall whet and sharpen them so as to make them penetrate, and teach and impress them diligently upon the [minds and] hearts of your children, and shall talk of them when you sit in your house and when you walk by the way, and when you lie down and when you rise up.

2 Tim. 3:16 Every Scripture is God-breathed (given by His inspiration) and profitable for instruction, for reproof and conviction of sin, for correction of error and discipline in obedience, [and] for training in righteousness (in holy living, in conformity to God's will in thought, purpose, and action),

2 Tim. 3:17 So that the man of God may be complete and proficient, well fitted and thoroughly equipped for every good work.

Eph. 5:19 Speak out to one another in psalms and hymns and spiritual songs, offering praise with voices [and instruments] and making melody with all your heart to the Lord,

Prov. 17:22 A happy heart is good medicine and a cheerful mind works healing, but a broken spirit dries up the bones.

Gal. 6:9 And let us not lose heart and grow weary and faint in acting nobly and doing right, for in due time and at the appointed season we shall reap, if we do not loosen and relax our courage and faint.

Is. 44:3 For I will pour water upon him who is thirsty, and floods upon the dry ground. I will pour My Spirit upon your offspring, and My blessing upon your descendants.

Is. 44:4 And they shall spring up among the grass like willows or poplars by the watercourses.

Praise

Ps. 113:3 From the rising of the sun to the going down of it and from east to west, the name of the Lord is to be praised!

Ps. 95:6 O come, let us worship and bow down, let us kneel before the Lord our Maker [in reverent praise and supplication].

Ps. 100:2 Serve the Lord with gladness! Come before His presence with singing!

Ps. 100:3 Know that the Lord is God! It is He Who has made us, not we ourselves [and we are His]! We are His people and the sheep of His pasture. [Eph. 2:10.]

Ps. 100:4 Enter into His gates with thanksgiving and
a thank offering and into His courts with praise! Be
thankful and say so to Him, bless and affectionately
praise His name!

Ps. 111:3 His work is honorable and glorious, and His
righteousness endures forever.

Ps. 138:2 I will worship toward Your holy temple and
praise Your name for Your loving-kindness and for
Your truth and faithfulness; for You have exalted
above all else Your name and Your word and You
have magnified Your word above all Your name!

Ps. 119:171 My lips shall pour forth praise [with thanksgiving and renewed trust] when You teach me Your
statutes.

Ps. 119:103 How sweet are Your words to my taste,
sweeter than honey to my mouth!

Ps. 134:2 Lift up your hands in holiness and to the
sanctuary and bless the Lord [affectionately and
gratefully praise Him]!

Ps. 86:12 I will confess and praise You, O Lord my
God, with my whole (united) heart; and I will glorify
Your name forevermore.

Ps. 34:1 [A Psalm] of David; when he pretended to be
insane before Abimelech, who drove him out, and he
went away. I WILL bless the Lord at all times; His
praise shall continually be in my mouth.

Ps. 21:13 Be exalted, Lord, in Your strength; we will
sing and praise Your power.

Ps. 28:7 The Lord is my Strength and my [impen-
etrable] Shield; my heart trusts in, relies on, and
confidently leans on Him, and I am helped; therefore
my heart greatly rejoices, and with my song will I
praise Him.

Rom. 4:20 No unbelief or distrust made him waver
concerning the promise of God, but he grew strong
and was empowered by faith as he gave praise and
glory to God,

Ps. 150:6 Let everything that has breath and every
breath of life praise the Lord! Praise the Lord!
(Hallelujah!)

Ps. 145:1 I WILL extol You, my God, O King; and I
will bless Your name forever and ever [with grateful,
affectionate praise].

Protection

Ps. 41:12 And as for me, You have upheld me in my
integrity and set me in Your presence forever.

Ps. 139:5 You have beset me and shut me in—behind
and before, and You have laid Your hand upon me.

Ruth 2:12 The Lord recompense you for what you have
done, and a full reward be given you by the Lord, the
God of Israel, under Whose wings you have come to
take refuge!

Ps. 145:18 The Lord is near to all who call upon Him,
to all who call upon Him sincerely and in truth.

Ps. 145:19 He will fulfill the desires of those who reverently and worshipfully fear Him; He also will hear
their cry and will save them.

Prov. 30:5 Every word of God is tried and purified;
He is a shield to those who trust and take refuge in
Him.

Prov. 18:10 The name of the Lord is a strong tower; the
[consistently] righteous man [upright and in right
standing with God] runs into it and is safe, high
[above evil] and strong.

Phil. 4:7 And God's peace [shall be yours, that tran-
quil state of a soul assured of its salvation through
Christ, and so fearing nothing from God and being
content with its earthly lot of whatever sort that
is, that peace] which transcends all understanding
shall garrison and mount guard over your hearts and
minds in Christ Jesus.

2 Chr. 20:17 You shall not need to fight in this battle;
take your positions, stand still, and see the deliverance of the Lord [Who is] with you, O Judah and
Jerusalem. Fear not nor be dismayed. Tomorrow go
out against them, for the Lord is with you.

Is. 59:19 So [as the result of the Messiah's interven-
tion] they shall [reverently] fear the name of the Lord
from the west, and His glory from the rising of the
sun. When the enemy shall come in like a flood, the
Spirit of the Lord will lift up a standard against him
and put him to flight [for He will come like a rushing
stream which the breath of the Lord drives].

2 Thess. 3:3 Yet the Lord is faithful, and He will
strengthen [you] and set you on a firm foundation
and guard you from the evil [one].

Ps. 91:2 I will say of the Lord, He is my Refuge and
my Fortress, my God; on Him I lean and rely, and
in Him I [confidently] trust!

Reconciliation

Rom. 5:1 THEREFORE, SINCE we are justified
[acquitted, declared righteous, and given a right
standing with God] through faith, let us have
peace with God through our Lord Jesus Christ [the
Messiah, the Anointed One].

Rom. 5:10 For if while we were enemies we were reconciled to God through the death of His Son, it is

much more [certain], now that we are reconciled,
that we shall be saved (daily delivered from sin's
dominion) through His [resurrection] life.

2 Cor 5:20 So we are Christ's ambassadors, God
making His appeal as it were through us. We [as
Christ's personal representatives] beg you for His
sake to lay hold of the divine favor [now offered you]
and be reconciled to God.

Col. 1:12 To the saints (the consecrated people of God)
and believing and faithful brethren in Christ who
are at Colossae: Grace (spiritual favor and blessing)
to you and [heart] peace from God our Father

Relationships . . .
as a Single Father

Mark 10:16 And He took them [the children up one by
one] in His arms and [fervently invoked a] blessing,
placing His hands upon them.

Heb. 12:9 Moreover, we have had earthly fathers who
disciplined us and we yielded and respected. Shall
we not much more cheerfully submit to the Father of
spirits and so [truly] live?

Heb. 12:10 For [our earthly fathers] disciplined us
for only a short period of time and chastised us as
seemed proper and good to them; but He disciplines
us for our certain good, that we may become sharers
in His own holiness.

Ps. 90:16 Let Your work [the signs of Your power] be
revealed to Your servants, and Your [glorious] majesty to their children.

Eph. 5:29 For no man ever hated his own flesh, but
nourishes and carefully protects and cherishes it, as
Christ does the church,

Relationships . . . as a Husband

Matt. 19:5 And said, For this reason a man shall leave his father and mother and shall be united firmly (joined inseparably) to his wife, and the two shall become one flesh.

Genesis 2:24 For this reason a man will leave his father and mother and be united to his wife, and they will become one flesh.

1 Peter 3:7 In the same way you married men should live considerately with [your wives], with an [a]intelligent recognition [of the marriage relation], honoring the woman as [physically] the weaker, but [realizing that you] are joint heirs of the grace (God's unmerited favor) of life, in order that your prayers may not be hindered and cut off. [Otherwise you cannot pray effectively.]

Colossians 3:19 Husbands, love your wives [be affectionate and sympathetic with them] and do not be harsh or bitter or resentful toward them.

Proverbs 18:22 He who finds a [true] wife finds a good thing and obtains favor from the Lord.

Eph. 5:21 Be subject to one another out of reverence for Christ (the Messiah, the Anointed One).

Eph. 5:23 For the husband is head of the wife as Christ is the Head of the church, Himself the Savior of [His] body.

Heb. 13:4 Let marriage be held in honor (esteemed worthy, precious, of great price, and especially dear) in all things. And thus let the marriage bed be undefiled (kept undishonored); for God will judge and punish the unchaste [all guilty of sexual vice] and adulterous.

1 Cor. 7:5 Do not refuse and deprive and defraud each other [of your due marital rights], except perhaps by

mutual consent for a time, so that you may devote
yourselves unhindered to prayer. But afterwards
resume marital relations, lest Satan tempt you [to
sin] through your lack of restraint of sexual desire.

Relationships . . . as Father of a Blended Family

Mark 10:16 And He took them [the children up one by
one] in His arms and [fervently invoked a] blessing,
placing His hands upon them.

James 1:5 If any of you is deficient in wisdom, let him
ask of the giving God [Who gives] to everyone
liberally and ungrudgingly, without reproaching or
faultfinding, and it will be given him.

Prov. 22:6 Train up a child in the way he should go
[and in keeping with his individual gift or bent], and
when he is old he will not depart from it.

James 2:1 MY BRETHREN, pay no servile regard
to people [show no prejudice, no partiality]. Do not
[attempt to] hold and practice the faith of our Lord
Jesus Christ [the Lord] of glory [together with snob-
bery]!

Ps. 139:23 Search me [thoroughly], O God, and know
my heart! Try me and know my thoughts!

Ps. 139:24 And see if there is any wicked or hurtful way
in me, and lead me in the way everlasting.

John 1:12 But to as many as did receive and welcome
Him, He gave the authority (power, privilege, right)
to become the children of God, that is, to those who
believe in (adhere to, trust in, and rely on) His name

Eph. 5:23 For the husband is head of the wife as Christ
is the Head of the church, Himself the Savior of
[His] body.

Deut. 5:16 Honor your father and your mother, as the Lord your God commanded you, that your days may be prolonged and that it may go well with you in the land which the Lord your God gives you.

Col. 3:20 Children, obey your parents in everything, for this is pleasing to the Lord.

Rom. 15:5 Now may the God Who gives the power of patient endurance (steadfastness) and Who supplies encouragement, grant you to live in such mutual harmony and such full sympathy with one another, in accord with Christ Jesus,

Rom. 15:7 Welcome and receive [to your hearts] one another, then, even as Christ has welcomed and received you, for the glory of God.

Eph. 2:14 For He is [Himself] our peace (our bond of unity and harmony). He has made us both [Jew and Gentile] one [body], and has broken down (destroyed, abolished) the hostile dividing wall between us,

1 Cor. 12:12 For just as the body is a unity and yet has many parts, and all the parts, though many, form [only] one body, so it is with Christ (the Messiah, the Anointed One).

Rom. 12:4 For as in one physical body we have many parts (organs, members) and all of these parts do not have the same function or use,

Rom. 12:5 So we, numerous as we are, are one body in Christ (the Messiah) and individually we are parts one of another [mutually dependent on one another].

Rom. 15:6 That together you may [unanimously] with united hearts and one voice, praise and glorify the God and Father of our Lord Jesus Christ (the Messiah).

Relationships . . . as a Widower

Eph. 5:29 For no man ever hated his own flesh, but nourishes and carefully protects and cherishes it, as Christ does the church,

Deut. 10:18 He executes justice for the fatherless and the widow, and loves the stranger or temporary resident and gives him food and clothing.

Ps. 37:7 Be still and rest in the Lord; wait for Him and patiently lean yourself upon Him; fret not yourself because of him who prospers in his way, because of the man who brings wicked devices to pass.

Ps. 37:25 I have been young and now am old, yet have I not seen the [uncompromisingly] righteous forsaken or their seed begging bread.

Releasing the Word of God

2 Tim. 2:15 Study and be eager and do your utmost to present yourself to God approved (tested by trial), a workman who has no cause to be ashamed, correctly analyzing and accurately dividing [rightly handling and skillfully teaching] the Word of Truth.

James 4:3 [Or] you do ask [God for them] and yet fail to receive, because you ask with wrong purpose and evil, selfish motives. Your intention is [when you get what you desire] to spend it in sensual pleasures.

Eccl. 5:2 Be not rash with your mouth, and let not your heart be hasty to utter a word before God. For God is in heaven, and you are on earth; therefore let your words be few.

Prov. 6:2 You are snared with the words of your lips, you are caught by the speech of your mouth.

Matt. 12:37 For by your words you will be justified and acquitted, and by your words you will be condemned and sentenced.

Luke 10:19 Behold! I have given you authority and power to trample upon serpents and scorpions, and [physical and mental strength and ability] over all the power that the enemy [possesses]; and nothing shall in any way harm you.

Matt. 6:6 But when you pray, go into your [most] private room, and, closing the door, pray to your Father, Who is in secret; and your Father, Who sees in secret, will reward you in the open.

Matt. 6:7 And when you pray, do not heap up phrases as the Gentiles do, for they think they will be heard for their much speaking.

Eph. 5:4 Let there be no filthiness nor foolish and sinful talk, nor coarse jesting, which are not fitting or becoming; but instead voice your thankfulness [to God].

Heb. 10:24 And let us consider and give attentive, continuous care to watching over one another, studying how we may stir up (stimulate and incite) to love and helpful deeds and noble activities,

Heb. 10:25 Not forsaking or neglecting to assemble together [as believers], as is the habit of some people, but admonishing (warning, urging, and encouraging) one another, and all the more faithfully as you see the day approaching.

Eph. 4:30 And do not grieve the Holy Spirit of God [do not offend or vex or sadden Him], by Whom you were sealed (marked, branded as God's own, secured) for the day of redemption (of final deliverance through Christ from evil and the consequences of sin).

Ps. 150:2 Praise Him for His mighty acts; praise Him according to the abundance of His greatness!

Ps. 111:2 The works of the Lord are great, sought out by all those who have delight in them.

Ps. 111:3 His work is honorable and glorious, and His righteousness endures forever.

Rom. 12:5 So we, numerous as we are, are one body in Christ (the Messiah) and individually we are parts one of another [mutually dependent on one another].

Col. 2:15 [God] disarmed the principalities and powers that were ranged against us and made a bold display and public example of them, in triumphing over them in Him and in it [the cross].

Ps. 84:11 For the Lord God is a Sun and Shield; the Lord bestows [present] grace and favor and [future] glory (honor, splendor, and heavenly bliss)! No good thing will He withhold from those who walk uprightly.

Ps. 84:12 O Lord of hosts, blessed (happy, fortunate, to be envied) is the man who trusts in You [leaning and believing on You, committing all and confidently looking to You, and that without fear or misgiving]!

Ps. 138:7 Though I walk in the midst of trouble, You will revive me; You will stretch forth Your hand against the wrath of my enemies, and Your right hand will save me.

Rev. 12:11 And they have overcome (conquered) him by means of the blood of the Lamb and by the utterance of their testimony, for they did not love and cling to life even when faced with death [holding their lives cheap till they had to die for their witnessing].

Deut. 28:3 Blessed shall you be in the city and blessed shall you be in the field.

Deut. 28:4 Blessed shall be the fruit of your body and the fruit of your ground and the fruit of your beasts, the increase of your cattle and the young of your flock.

Deut. 28:5 Blessed shall be your basket and your kneading trough.

Deut. 28:6 Blessed shall you be when you come in and blessed shall you be when you go out.

Deut. 28:7 The Lord shall cause your enemies who rise up against you to be defeated before your face; they shall come out against you one way and flee before you seven ways.

Deut. 28:8 The Lord shall command the blessing upon you in your storehouse and in all that you undertake. And He will bless you in the land which the Lord your God gives you.

Deut. 28:9 The Lord will establish you as a people holy to Himself, as He has sworn to you, if you keep the commandments of the Lord your God and walk in His ways.

Deut. 28:10 And all people of the earth shall see that you are called by the name [and in the presence of] the Lord, and they shall be afraid of you.

Deut. 28:11 And the Lord shall make you have a surplus of prosperity, through the fruit of your body, of your livestock, and of your ground, in the land which the Lord swore to your fathers to give you.

Deut. 28:12 The Lord shall open to you His good treasury, the heavens, to give the rain of your land in its season and to bless all the work of your hands; and you shall lend to many nations, but you shall not borrow.

Deut. 28:13 And the Lord shall make you the head, and not the tail; and you shall be above only, and you shall not be beneath, if you heed the commandments of the Lord your God which I command you this day and are watchful to do them.

2 Cor. 12:9 But He said to me, My grace (My favor and loving-kindness and mercy) is enough for you [sufficient against any danger and enables you to bear the trouble manfully]; for My strength and

power are made perfect (fulfilled and completed) and show themselves most effective in [your] weakness.

1 John 4:4 Little children, you are of God [you belong to Him] and have [already] defeated and overcome them [the agents of the antichrist], because He Who lives in you is greater (mightier) than he who is in the world.

John 14:17 The Spirit of Truth, Whom the world cannot receive (welcome, take to its heart), because it does not see Him or know and recognize Him. But you know and recognize Him, for He lives with you [constantly] and will be in you.

2 Tim. 1:14 Guard and keep [with the greatest care] the precious and excellently adapted [Truth] which has been entrusted [to you], by the [help of the] Holy Spirit Who makes His home in us.

1 John 2:27 But as for you, the anointing which you received from Him abides in you; [so] then you have no need that anyone should instruct you. But just as His anointing teaches you concerning everything and is true and is no falsehood, so you must abide in Him [being rooted in Him, knit to Him], just as His anointing has taught you [to do].

1 Cor. 2:15 But the spiritual man tries all things [he examines, investigates, inquires into, questions, and discerns all things], yet is himself to be put on trial and judged by no one [he can read the meaning of everything, but no one can properly discern or appraise or get an insight into him].

1 Cor. 2:16 For who has known or understood the mind (the counsels and purposes) of the Lord so as to guide and instruct Him and give Him knowledge? But we have the mind of Christ (the Messiah) and do hold the thoughts (feelings and purposes) of His heart.

Ps. 32:8 I [the Lord] will instruct you and teach you in the way you should go; I will counsel you with My eye upon you.

Restoration

Gal. 2:20 I have been crucified with Christ [in Him I have shared His crucifixion]; it is no longer I who live, but Christ (the Messiah) lives in me; and the life I now live in the body I live by faith in (by adherence to and reliance on and complete trust in) the Son of God, Who loved me and gave Himself up for me.

Gal. 3:26 For in Christ Jesus you are all sons of God through faith.

John 5:24 I assure you, most solemnly I tell you, the person whose ears are open to My words and believes and trusts in and clings to and relies on Him Who sent Me has eternal life. And he does not come into judgment [does not incur sentence of judgment, will not come under condemnation], but he has already passed over out of death into life.

Rom. 5:1 THEREFORE, SINCE we are justified (acquitted, declared righteous, and given a right standing with God) through faith, let us [grasp the fact that we] have [the peace of reconciliation to hold and to enjoy] peace with God through our Lord Jesus Christ (the Messiah, the Anointed One).

Rom. 5:10 For if while we were enemies we were reconciled to God through the death of His Son, it is much more [certain], now that we are reconciled, that we shall be saved (daily delivered from sin's dominion) through His [resurrection] life.

Rom. 8:1 THEREFORE, [there is] now no condemnation for those who are in Christ Jesus, who live

[and] walk not after the dictates of the flesh, but after the dictates of the Spirit

Rom. 12:2 Do not be conformed to this world, , but be transformed [changed] by the [entire] renewal of your mind, so that you may prove what is the good and acceptable and perfect will of God, even the thing which is good and acceptable and perfect.

Joel 2:25 And I will restore or replace for you the years that the locusts have eaten—the hopping locust, the stripping locust, and the crawling locust, My great army which I sent among you.

Joel 2:26 And you shall eat in plenty and be satisfied and praise the name of the Lord, your God, Who has dealt wondrously with you. And My people shall never be put to shame.

Phil. 1:6 And I am convinced and sure of this very thing, that He Who began a good work in you will continue until the day of Jesus Christ [right up to the time of His return], developing [that good work] and perfecting and bringing it to full completion in you.

2 Cor. 5:18 But all things are from God, Who through Jesus Christ reconciled us to Himself [received us into favor, brought us into harmony with Himself] and gave to us the ministry of reconciliation [that by word and deed we might aim to bring others into harmony with Him].

2 Co 5:20 So we are Christ's ambassadors, God making His appeal as it were through us. We [as Christ's personal representatives] beg you for His sake to lay hold of the divine favor and be reconciled to God.

Ps. 23:3 He refreshes and restores my life (my self); He leads me in the paths of righteousness [uprightness and right standing with Him—not for my earning it, but] for His name's sake.

Ps. 80:3 Restore us again, O God; and cause Your face to shine [in pleasure and approval on us], and we shall be saved!

Ezek. 36:26 A new heart will I give you and a new spirit will I put within you, and I will take away the stony heart out of your flesh and give you a heart of flesh.

Col. 1:2 To the saints and believing and faithful brethren in Christ who are at Colossae: Grace to you and [heart] peace from God our Father.

Is. 58:8 Then shall your light break forth like the morning, and your healing shall spring forth speedily; your righteousness shall go before you [conducting you to peace and prosperity], and the glory of the Lord shall be your rear guard

Servanthood

Ps. 100:2 Serve the Lord with gladness! Come before His presence with singing!

Eph. 2:10 For we are God's [own] handiwork (His workmanship), recreated in Christ Jesus, [born anew] that we may do those good works which God predestined (planned beforehand) for us [taking paths which He prepared ahead of time], that we should walk in them [living the good life which He prearranged and made ready for us to live].

Matt. 5:14 You are the light of the world. A city set on a hill cannot be hidden.

Matt. 5:15 Nor do men light a lamp and put it under a peck measure, but on a lampstand, and it gives light to all in the house.

Matt. 5:16 Let your light so shine before men that they may see your moral excellence and your praiseworthy, noble, and good deeds and recognize and honor and praise and glorify your Father Who is in heaven.

Rom. 12:1 I APPEAL to you therefore, brethren, and beg of you in view of [all] the mercies of God, to make a decisive dedication of your bodies [presenting all your members and faculties] as a living sacrifice, holy (devoted, consecrated) and well pleasing to God, which is your reasonable (rational, intelligent) service and spiritual worship.

Col. 3:23 Whatever may be your task, work at it heartily (from the soul), as [something done] for the Lord and not for men,

Col. 3:24 Knowing [with all certainty] that it is from the Lord [and not from men] that you will receive the inheritance which is your [real] reward. [The One Whom] you are actually serving [is] the Lord Christ (the Messiah).

Prov. 14:21 He who despises his neighbor sins [against God, his fellow man, and himself], but happy (blessed and fortunate) is he who is kind and merciful to the poor.

Gal. 5:13 For you, brethren, were [indeed] called to freedom; only [do not let your] freedom be an incentive to your flesh and an opportunity or excuse [for selfishness], but through love you should serve one another.

Rom. 12:13 Contribute to the needs of God's people [sharing in the necessities of the saints]; pursue the practice of hospitality.

2 Cor. 1:4 Who comforts us in every trouble, so that we may also be able to comfort those who are in any kind of trouble or distress, with the comfort with which we ourselves are comforted by God.

2 Cor. 9:8 And God is able to make all grace come to you in abundance, so that you may always and under all circumstances and whatever the need be self-sufficient [possessing enough to require no aid or support and furnished in abundance for every good work and charitable donation].

John 12:26 If anyone serves Me, he must continue to follow Me [to cleave steadfastly to Me, conform wholly to My example in living and, if need be, in dying] and wherever I am, there will My servant be also. If anyone serves Me, the Father will honor him.

Gal. 6:9 And let us not lose heart and grow weary and faint in acting nobly and doing right, for in due time and at the appointed season we shall reap, if we do not loosen and relax our courage and faint.

Is. 40:31 But those who wait for the Lord shall change and renew their strength and power; they shall lift their wings and mount up [close to God] as eagles; they shall run and not be weary, they shall walk and not faint or become tired. [Heb. 12:1-3.]

1 Tim. 1:12 I give thanks to Him Who has granted me strength and made me able, Christ Jesus our Lord, because He has judged and counted me faithful and trustworthy, appointing me to the ministry.

2 Tim. 2:21 So whoever cleanses himself [from what is ignoble and unclean, who separates himself from contact with contaminating and corrupting influences] will [then himself] be a vessel set apart and useful for honorable and noble purposes, consecrated and profitable to the Master, fit and ready for any good work.

Spirit of Joy

Luke 6:23 Rejoice and be glad at such a time and exult and leap for joy, for behold, your reward is rich and great and strong and intense and abundant in heaven; for even so their forefathers treated the prophets.

Luke 10:20 Nevertheless, do not rejoice at this, that the spirits are subject to you, but rejoice that your names are enrolled in heaven.

Ps. 71:23 My lips shall shout for joy when I sing praises to You, and my inner being, which You have redeemed.

Ps. 35:9 Then I shall be joyful in the Lord; I shall rejoice in His deliverance.

Jer. 15:16 Your words were found, and I ate them; and Your words were to me a joy and the rejoicing of my heart, for I am called by Your name, O Lord God of hosts.

Acts 2:38 And Peter answered them, Repent (change your views and purpose to accept the will of God in your inner selves instead of rejecting it) and be baptized, every one of you, in the name of Jesus Christ for the forgiveness of and release from your sins; and you shall receive the gift of the Holy Spirit.

Gal. 5:22 But the fruit of the [Holy] Spirit [the work which His presence within accomplishes] is love, joy, peace, patience, kindness, goodness, faithfulness,

Is. 29:19 The meek also shall increase their joy in the Lord, and the poor among men shall rejoice and exult in the Holy One of Israel.

Eccl. 2:26 For to the person who pleases Him God gives wisdom and knowledge and joy; but to the sinner He gives the work of gathering and heaping

up, that he may give to one who pleases God. This
also is vanity and a striving after the wind and a
feeding on it.

Col. 1:10 That you may walk in a manner worthy
of the Lord, fully pleasing to Him and desiring to
please Him in all things, bearing fruit in every good
work and steadily growing and increasing in and by
the knowledge of God.

Heb. 1:9 You have loved righteousness [You have
delighted in integrity, virtue, and uprightness in
purpose, thought, and action] and You have hated
lawlessness [injustice and iniquity]. Therefore God,
[even] Your God (Godhead), has anointed You
with the oil of exultant joy and gladness above and
beyond Your companions.

Neh. 8:10 Then [Ezra] told them, Go your way, eat
the fat, drink the sweet drink, and send portions to
him for whom nothing is prepared; for this day is
holy to our Lord. And be not grieved and depressed,
for the joy of the Lord is your strength and strong-
hold.

Ps. 97:11 Light is sown for the righteous and strewn
along their pathway, and joy for the upright in heart.

Is. 49:13 Sing for joy, O heavens, and be joyful, O
earth, and break forth into singing, O mountains!
For the Lord has comforted His people and will have
compassion upon His afflicted.

Ps. 5:11 But let all those who take refuge and put their
trust in You rejoice; let them ever sing and shout
for joy, because You make a covering over them and
defend them; let those also who love Your name be
joyful in You and be in high spirits.

Is. 12:2 Behold, God, my salvation! I will trust and not
be afraid, for the Lord God is my strength and song;
yes, He has become my salvation.

Ps. 21:6 For You make him to be blessed and a blessing forever; You make him exceedingly glad with the joy of Your presence.

Ps. 31:19 Oh, how great is Your goodness, which You have laid up for those who fear, revere and worship You, goodness which You have wrought for those who trust and take refuge in You before the sons of men!

Ps. 31:20 In the secret place of Your presence You hide them from the plots of men; You keep them secretly in Your pavilion from the strife of tongues.

Spiritual Warfare

Luke 10:19 Behold! I have given you authority and power to trample upon serpents and scorpions, and |physical and mental strength| over all the power that the enemy |possesses|; and nothing shall in any way harm you.

Is. 41:10 Fear not, for I am with you; do not look around you in terror and be dismayed, for I am your God. I will strengthen and harden you to difficulties, yes, I will help you; yes, I will hold you up and retain you with My right hand of rightness and justice.

Is. 54:17 But no weapon that is formed against you shall prosper, and every tongue that shall rise against you in judgment you shall show to be in the wrong. This |peace, righteousness, security, triumph over opposition| is the heritage of the servants of the Lord; this is the righteousness or the vindication which they obtain from Me |this is that which I impart to them as their justification|, says the Lord.

Rev. 12:11 And they have overcome him by means of the blood of the Lamb and by the utterance of their testimony, for they did not love and cling to life even when faced with death.

John 10:10 The thief comes only in order to steal and kill and destroy. I came that they may have and enjoy life, and have it in abundance.

1 Peter 5:8 Be well balanced, be vigilant and cautious at all times; for that enemy of yours, the devil, roams around like a lion roaring, seeking someone to seize upon and devour.

Ps. 60:12 Through God we shall do valiantly, for He it is Who shall tread down our adversaries.

1 Cor. 10:13 For no temptation, has overtaken you and laid hold on you that is not common to man [that is, no temptation or trial has come to you that is beyond human resistance and that is not adjusted and adapted and belonging to human experience, and such as man can bear]. But God is faithful, and He will not let you be tempted and tried and assayed beyond your ability and strength of resistance and power to endure, but with the temptation He will also provide the way out, that you may be capable and strong and powerful to bear up under it patiently.

2 Cor. 10:4 For the weapons of our warfare are not physical , but they are mighty before God for the overthrow and destruction of strongholds,

Ps. 61:3 For You have been a shelter and a refuge for me, a strong tower against the adversary.

Ps. 46:1 To the Chief Musician. [A Psalm] of the sons of Korah, set to treble voices. A song. GOD IS our Refuge and Strength, a very present and well-proved help in trouble.

Ps. 145:18 The Lord is near to all who call upon Him, to all who call upon Him sincerely and in truth.

Ps. 145:19 He will fulfill the desires of those who reverently and worshipfully fear Him; He also will hear their cry and will save them.

James 1:12 Blessed is the man who is patient under
trial and stands up under temptation, for when he
has stood the test and been approved, he will receive
[the victor's] crown of life which God has promised
to those who love Him.

1 Cor. 15:57 But thanks be to God, Who gives us the
victory [making us conquerors] through our Lord
Jesus Christ.

Submission

2 Cor. 5:7 For we walk by faith [we regulate our lives
and conduct ourselves by our conviction or belief
respecting man's relationship to God and divine
things, with trust and holy fervor; thus we walk] not
by sight or appearance.

Prov. 3:5 Lean on, trust in, and be confident in the Lord
with all your heart and mind and do not rely on your
own insight or understanding.

Prov. 3:6 In all your ways know, recognize and
acknowledge Him, and He will direct and make
straight and plain your paths.

Phil. 2:5 Let this same attitude and purpose and [hum-
ble] mind be in you which was in Christ Jesus:

Prov. 8:8 All the words of my mouth are righteous
(upright and in right standing with God); there is
nothing contrary to truth or crooked in them.

Prov. 15:26 The thoughts of the wicked are shamefully
vile and exceedingly offensive to the Lord, but the
words of the pure are pleasing words to Him.

Heb. 12:7 You must submit to and endure [correction]
for discipline; God is dealing with you as with sons.
For what son is there whom his father does not
[thus] train and correct and discipline?

Heb. 12:10 For [our earthly fathers] disciplined us for only a short period of time and chastised us as seemed proper and good to them; but He disciplines us for our certain good, that we may become sharers in His own holiness.

1 Pet. 2:13 Be submissive to every human institution and authority for the sake of the Lord, whether it be to the emperor as supreme,

Col. 3:20 Children, obey your parents in everything, for this is pleasing to the Lord.

Heb. 13:17 Obey your spiritual leaders and submit to them, for they are constantly keeping watch over your souls and guarding your spiritual welfare, as men who will have to render an account. [Do your part to] let them do this with gladness and not with sighing and groaning, for that would not be profitable to you [either].

Col. 3:22 Servants, obey in everything those who are your earthly masters, not only when their eyes are on you as pleasers of men, but in simplicity of purpose because of your reverence for the Lord and as a sincere expression of your devotion to Him.

Rom. 12:10 Love one another with brotherly affection, giving precedence and showing honor to one another.

Heb. 11:6 But without faith it is impossible to please and be satisfactory to Him. For whoever would come near to God must [necessarily] believe that God exists and that He is the rewarder of those who earnestly and diligently seek Him [out].

James 4:7 So be subject to God. Resist the devil, and he will flee from you.

Phil. 2:5 Let this same attitude and purpose and [humble] mind be in you which was in Christ Jesus: [Let Him be your example in humility:]

2 Cor 5:7 For we walk by faith not by sight or appearance.

Prov 3:5 Lean on, trust in, and be confident in the Lord with all your heart and mind and do not rely on your own insight or understanding.

Prov 3:6 In all your ways know, recognize and acknowledge Him, and He will direct and make straight and plain your paths.

Waiting for a Spouse

Ps. 37:4 Delight yourself also in the Lord, and He will give you the desires and secret petitions of your heart.

Ps. 37:5 Commit your way to the Lord; trust also in Him and He will bring it to pass.

1 John 5:14 And this is the confidence (the assurance, the privilege of boldness) which we have in Him: [we are sure] that if we ask anything according to His will, He listens to and hears us.

1 John 5:15 And if we know that He listens to us in whatever we ask, we also know that we have the requests made of Him.

2 Cor. 6:14 Do not be unequally yoked with unbelievers [do not make mismatched alliances with them or come under a different yoke with them, inconsistent with your faith]. For what partnership have right living and right standing with God with iniquity and lawlessness? Or how can light have fellowship with darkness?

Eph. 5:31 For this reason a man shall leave his father and his mother and shall be joined to his wife, and the two shall become one flesh.

Eph. 5:25 Husbands, love your wives, as Christ loved the Church and gave Himself up for her,

Eph. 5:29 For no man ever hated his own flesh, but nourishes and carefully protects and cherishes it, as Christ does the Church,

Matt. 19:6 So they are no longer two, but one flesh. What therefore God has joined together, let not man put asunder.

Matt. 6:34 So do not worry or be anxious about tomorrow, for tomorrow will have worries and anxieties of its own. Sufficient for each day is its own trouble.

Is. 26:3 You will guard him and keep him in perfect and constant peace whose mind is stayed on You, because he commits himself to You, leans on You and hopes confidently in You.

Is. 34:16 Seek out the book of the Lord and read: not one of these shall fail, none shall want and lack her mate. For the mouth [of the Lord] has commanded, and His Spirit has gathered them.

Phil. 4:6 Do not fret or have any anxiety about anything, but in every circumstance and in everything, by prayer and petition, with thanksgiving, continue to make your wants known to God.

Phil. 4:7 And God's peace which transcends all understanding shall garrison and mount guard over your hearts and minds in Christ Jesus.

Jer. 29:11 For I know the thoughts and plans that I have for you, says the Lord, thoughts and plans for welfare and peace and not for evil, to give you hope in your final outcome.

Rom. 15:13 May the God of your hope so fill you with all joy and peace in believing that by the power of the Holy Spirit you may abound and be overflowing with hope.

Walking in Faith

Gal. 3:29 And if you belong to Christ, then you are Abraham's offspring and [spiritual] heirs according to promise.

Gal. 2:20 I have been crucified with Christ; it is no longer I who live, but Christ (the Messiah) lives in me; and the life I now live in the body I live by faith in the Son of God, Who loved me and gave Himself up for me.

2 Cor. 5:7 For we walk by faith not by sight or appearance.

Prov. 3:5 Lean on, trust in, and be confident in the Lord with all your heart and mind and do not rely on your own insight or understanding.

Prov. 3:6 In all your ways know, recognize and acknowledge Him, and He will direct and make straight and plain your paths.

Eph. 1:17 [For I always pray to] the God of our Lord Jesus Christ, the Father of glory, that He may grant you a spirit of wisdom and revelation in the knowledge of Him,

Rom. 10:17 So faith comes by hearing [what is told], and what is heard comes by the preaching [of the message that came from the lips] of Christ (the Messiah Himself).

2 Tim. 2:22 Shun youthful lusts and flee from them, and aim at and pursue righteousness, faith, love, [and] peace in fellowship with all who call upon the Lord out of a pure heart.

Prov. 8:8 All the words of my mouth are righteous; there is nothing contrary to truth or crooked in them.

Prov. 15:26 The thoughts of the wicked are shamefully vile and exceedingly offensive to the Lord, but the words of the pure are pleasing words to Him.

Ps. 34:14 Depart from evil and do good; seek, inquire for, and crave peace and pursue [go after] it!

Luke 1:37 For with God nothing is ever impossible and no word from God shall be without power or impossible of fulfillment.

Heb. 11:1 NOW FAITH is the assurance of the things hoped for, being the proof of things not seen and the conviction of their reality.

Matt. 21:22 And whatever you ask for in prayer, having faith and [really] believing, you will receive.

Mark 11:24 For this reason I am telling you, whatever you ask for in prayer, believe that it is granted to you, and you will [get it].

Luke 11:10 For everyone who asks and keeps on asking receives; and he who seeks and keeps on seeking finds; and to him who knocks and keeps on knocking, the door shall be opened.

1 John 5:15 And if [since] we know that He listens to us in whatever we ask, we also that we have the requests made of Him.

Jude 1:20 But you, beloved, build yourselves up on your most holy faith, praying in the Holy Spirit;

Jude 1:21 Guard and keep yourselves in the love of God; expect and patiently wait for the mercy of our Lord Jesus Christ (the Messiah)—[which will bring you] unto life eternal.

Phil. 1:6 And I am convinced and sure of this very thing, that He Who began a good work in you will continue until the day of Jesus Christ [right up to the time of His return], developing and perfecting and bringing it to full completion in you.

Heb. 11:6 But without faith it is impossible to please and be satisfactory to Him. For whoever would come near to God must believe that God exists and that He is the rewarder of those who earnestly and diligently seek Him [out].

1 Cor. 7:35 Now I say this for your own welfare and profit, not to put restraint upon you, but to promote what is seemly and in good order and to secure your undistracted and undivided devotion to the Lord.

Wisdom

Prov. 3:13 Happy is the man who finds skillful and godly Wisdom, and the man who gets understanding,

Prov. 2:4 If you seek [Wisdom] as for silver and search for skillful and godly Wisdom as for hidden treasures,

Prov. 2:5 Then you will understand the reverent and worshipful fear of the Lord and find the knowledge of [our omniscient] God. [Prov. 1:7.]

Prov. 2:6 For the Lord gives skillful and godly Wisdom; from His mouth come knowledge and understanding.

Prov. 2:7 He hides away sound and godly Wisdom and stores it for the righteous; He is a shield to those who walk uprightly and in integrity,

Prov. 8:35 For whoever finds me [Wisdom] finds life and draws forth and obtains favor from the Lord.

James 1:5 If any of you is deficient in wisdom, let him ask of the giving God [Who gives] to everyone liberally and ungrudgingly, without reproaching or faultfinding, and it will be given him.

Jer. 33:3 Call to Me and I will answer you and show you great and mighty things, fenced in and hidden, which you do not know.

Prov. 3:14 For the gaining of it is better than the gaining of silver, and the profit of it better than fine gold.

Prov. 3:15 Skillful and godly Wisdom is more precious than rubies; and nothing you can wish for is to be compared to her.

Prov. 3:16 Length of days is in her right hand, and in her left hand are riches and honor.

Prov. 3:17 Her ways are highways of pleasantness, and all her paths are peace.

Prov. 3:18 She is a tree of life to those who lay hold on her; and happy is everyone who holds her fast.

Prov. 4:6 Forsake not [Wisdom], and she will keep, defend and protect you; love her, and she will guard you.

Prov. 4:8 Prize Wisdom highly and exalt her, and she will exalt and promote you; she will bring you to honor when you embrace her.

James 3:17 But the wisdom from above is first of all pure; then it is peace-loving, courteous [considerate, gentle]. [It is willing to] yield to reason, full of compassion and good fruits; it is wholehearted and straightforward, impartial and unfeigned.

Prov. 7:4 Say to skillful and godly Wisdom, You are my sister, and regard understanding or insight as your intimate friend—

Workplace

Eph. 2:10 For we are God's handiwork, recreated in Christ Jesus, that we may do those good works which God predestined for us, that we should walk in them.

Phil. 4:13 I have strength for all things in Christ Who empowers me.

2 Thess. 2:16 Now may our Lord Jesus Christ Himself
and God our Father, Who loved us and gave us
everlasting consolation and encouragement and
well-founded hope through [His] grace,

2 Thess. 2:17 Comfort and encourage your hearts and
strengthen them [make them steadfast and keep
them unswerving] in every good work and word.

2 Cor. 9:8 And God is able to make all grace come
to you in abundance, so that you may always and
under all circumstances and whatever the need be
self-sufficient.

Eccl. 9:10 Whatever your hand finds to do, do it with
all your might, for there is no work or device or
knowledge or wisdom in Sheol (the place of the
dead), where you are going.

Col. 3:17 And whatever you do [no matter what it is]
in word or deed, do everything in the name of the
Lord Jesus and in [dependence upon] His Person,
giving praise to God the Father through Him.

Eph. 6:5 Servants (slaves), be obedient to those who
are your physical masters, having respect for them
and eager concern to please them, in singleness of
motive and with all your heart, as [service] to Christ
[Himself]—

Eph. 6:6 Not in the way of eye-service and only to
please men, but as servants of Christ, doing the will
of God heartily and with your whole soul;

Eph. 6:7 Rendering service readily with goodwill, as to
the Lord and not to men,

Eph. 6:8 Knowing that for whatever good anyone does,
he will receive his reward from the Lord, whether he
is slave or free.

Titus 2:9 [Tell] bond servants to be submissive to their
masters, to be pleasing and give satisfaction in every
way. [Warn them] not to talk back or contradict,

Titus 2:10 Nor to steal by taking things of small value, but to prove themselves truly loyal and entirely reliable and faithful throughout, so that in everything they may be an ornament and do credit to the teaching [which is] from and about God our Savior.

Prov. 25:13 Like the cold of snow in the time of harvest, so is a faithful messenger to those who send him; for he refreshes the life of his masters.

Prov. 16:3 Roll your works upon the Lord [commit and trust them wholly to Him; He will cause your thoughts to become agreeable to His will, and] so shall your plans be established and succeed.

Ps. 37:5 Commit your way to the Lord; trust also in Him and He will bring it to pass.

Ps. 37:6 And He will make your uprightness and right standing with God go forth as the light, and your justice and cause as [the shining sun of] the noonday.

1 Thess. 4:11 To make it your ambition and definitely endeavor to live quietly and peacefully, to mind your own affairs, and to work with your hands, as we charged you,

1 Thess. 4:12 So that you may bear yourselves becomingly and be correct and honorable and command the respect of the outside world, being dependent on nobody and having need of nothing.

Phil. 2:14 Do all things without grumbling and faultfinding and complaining and questioning and doubting

Phil. 2:15 That you may show yourselves to be blameless and guileless, innocent and uncontaminated, children of God without blemish in the midst of a crooked and wicked generation, among whom you are seen as bright lights in the [dark] world,

Gal. 6:9 And let us not lose heart and grow weary and faint in acting nobly and doing right, for in due time and at the appointed season we shall reap, if we do not loosen and relax our courage and faint.

Is. 40:28 Have you not known? Have you not heard? The everlasting God, the Lord, the Creator of the ends of the earth, does not faint or grow weary; there is no searching of His understanding.

Is. 40:29 He gives power to the faint and weary, and to him who has no might He increases strength [causing it to multiply and making it to abound].

Is. 40:30 Even youths shall faint and be weary, and [selected] young men shall feebly stumble and fall exhausted;

Is. 40:31 But those who wait for the Lord shall change and renew their strength and power; they shall lift their wings and mount up as eagles; they shall run and not be weary, they shall walk and not faint or become tired.

Prov. 16:7 When a man's ways please the Lord, He makes even his enemies to be at peace with him.

Prov. 12:14 From the fruit of his words a man shall be satisfied with good, and the work of a man's hands shall come back to him.

Prov. 14:23 In all labor there is profit, but idle talk leads only to poverty.

Prov. 27:18 Whoever tends the fig tree shall eat its fruit; so he who patiently and faithfully guards and heeds his master shall be honored.

Eccl. 3:13 And also that every man should eat and drink and enjoy the good of all his labor—it is the gift of God.

Worship

Rev. 4:8 And the four living creatures, individually having six wings, were full of eyes all over and within and day and night they never stop saying, Holy, holy, holy is the Lord God Almighty (Omnipotent), Who was and Who is and Who is to come.

Is. 6:3 And one cried to another and said, Holy, holy, holy is the Lord of hosts; the whole earth is full of His glory!

Ps. 29:2 Give to the Lord the glory due to His name; worship the Lord in the beauty of holiness or in holy array.

Ps. 95:6 O come, let us worship and bow down, let us kneel before the Lord our Maker

Ps. 95:7a For He is our God and we are the people of His pasture and the sheep of His hand.

Heb. 3:1 SO THEN, brethren, consecrated and set apart for God, who share in the heavenly calling, consider Jesus, the Apostle and High Priest Whom we confessed

Eph. 3:12 In Whom, because of our faith in Him, we dare to have the boldness of free access

John 4:24 God is a Spirit and those who worship Him must worship Him in spirit and in truth (reality).

Rev. 4:11 Worthy are You, our Lord and God, to receive the glory and the honor and dominion, for You created all things; by Your will they were and were created.

Rev. 5:12 Saying in a loud voice, Deserving is the Lamb, Who was sacrificed, to receive all the power and riches and wisdom and might and honor and majesty and blessing!

1 Tim. 2:8 I desire therefore that in every place men should pray, without anger or quarreling or resentment or doubt [in their minds], lifting up holy hands.

Ps. 34:1 [A Psalm] of David; when he pretended to be insane before Abimelech, who drove him out, and he went away. I WILL bless the Lord at all times; His praise shall continually be in my mouth.

Rev. 7:10 In a loud voice they cried, saying, [Our] salvation is due to our God, Who is seated on the throne, and to the Lamb [to Them we owe our deliverance]!

Ps. 89:1 A skillful song, or a didactic or reflective poem, of Ethan the Ezrahite. I WILL sing of the mercy and loving-kindness of the Lord forever; with my mouth will I make known Your faithfulness from generation to generation.

NOTES

1. Webster's New Universal Unabridged Dictionary (New York: Barnes & Noble Books, 1996 by Random House Value Publishing, Inc)   1543

2. Derek Prince, The Power of Proclamation (South Pacific: Derek Prince Ministries, 2002)   6

3. Ibid., 108

4. Adapted from http://www.gospel truth.net/1859-51Penny_Pulpit/ indexpp.htm, The Promises of God, a Sermon preached on Friday evening, May 17, 1850, by the Rev. C. G. Finney (of America) at the Tabernacle, Moorfields

5. Derek Prince, The Power of Proclamation (South Pacific: Derek Prince Ministries, 2002)   109

6. Inspired by Illustrations Unlimited by James S. Hewett, 246